The Truth About

Jihad

The Truth About
Jihad

Maulana Yahya Nomani

English Translation
Yoginder Sikand

Vitasta

Vitasta Publishing Pvt. Ltd.
New Delhi

Published by
Renu Kaul Verma for
Vitasta Publishing Pvt. Ltd.
2/15, Ansari Road, Daryaganj,
New Delhi - 110 002

ISBN 978-93-80828-10-7

Cover Design and Layout by Vitasta Publishing Pvt. Ltd.

Contents

Preface

The Islamic doctrine of jihad has for long been a source of debate and controversy. An enormous number of books have been written on the subject, by Muslims and non-Muslims alike. Jihad remains at the heart of contemporary discussions about Islam and its place in the modern world and about Islamic teachings with regard to people of other faiths.

Some months ago, I chanced upon an Urdu book titled *Al-Jihad* written by a Lucknow-based Islamic scholar, Maulana Yahya Nomani. So fascinating did I find his book that once I began reading it, I could not put it down till I had finished it. Although I had read several books in English and Urdu before on the issue of jihad, this book struck me as quite distinct. Written by a young scholar trained in a traditional Indian *madrasa*, it seemed to appeal to Muslims as well as non-Muslims alike. It was equally critical of portrayals of jihad by Islamophobic scholars as being allegedly akin to terrorism as it was of radical self-styled Islamists, who believe it to be a license for indiscriminate slaughter of non-

Muslims as well as Muslims who do not subscribe to their vision of Islam. While I did not agree with everything that the author had to say, I felt that on the whole, the book made a valuable contribution to longstanding and still on-going debates about the doctrine of jihad. I believed that the book definitely deserved a much larger audience, and that is why I decided to translate it into English after seeking permission from the author.

Some salient issues that this book raises are the concept and purposes of jihad; the limits and rules governing jihad; the conditions under which armed jihad may be resorted to; the various non-violent forms of jihad; the treatment of non-Muslim combatants and non-combatants or civilians during armed jihad; the need for the contextual revision of certain rules related to jihad that are contained in the medieval corpus of *fiqh* or Muslim jurisprudence; the impermissibility of proxy war and communal conflict in the name of jihad; the duties and responsibilities of Muslim citizens or residents of non-Muslim states; and Islamic teachings about relations between Muslims and followers of other faiths.

Yoginder Sikand

Foreword

This book is an English translation of my Urdu book titled *Al-Jihad*. Many people, including my mentor, Maulana Atiq ur-Rahman Sambhali, Professor Syed Salman Nadwi, and other noted *ulema*, repeatedly insisted that it should come out in English in order to reach out to the wider, English-speaking public—not just to Muslims but also others who wish to understand the truth about jihad.

The Islamic concept of jihad has been greatly misunderstood. It has even been deliberately misinterpreted, particularly by Western writers, in order to damage the image of Islam and Muslims. The American authorities must surely be aware of the actual perpetrators of the attacks of 9/11, but after that incident, a huge propaganda offensive was launched to give jihad a bad name and to justify Western imperialist offensives against Muslims and occupation of Muslim lands, as in Iraq and Afghanistan. Present-day conflicts between Muslims and the West have their roots in the colonial age, and have now developed into proxy occupation of Muslim countries. The horrendous crimes committed by Western powers in the course of their naked occupation of Iraq and Afghanistan in the name of combating jihad have, naturally, led to heightened anger among Muslims. Even in Europe and America itself, a lot of peace-loving non-Muslims have stridently protested against these policies and atrocities. However, Western governments and the mass media have, through their massive propaganda machine, tried to brutally crush voices that cry out for justice. In this situation, it is not surprising that this continuing wave of oppression has inflamed a section of the Muslim youth. Their youthful zeal did not permit them to take cognizance of the demands of wisdom and practical realities. Consequently, some of them resorted to deviant behaviour and acts, inspired by extremist thinking in the name of jihad. Goaded by immense grief and pain, they began considering such acts as jihad that have no sanction whatsoever in the Islamic *Shari'ah*. The conditions under which they laboured also gave rise to the ideology of extremism.

This unfortunate situation requires that the Islamic concept of jihad be properly interpreted and explained afresh in accordance with the *Shari'ah* so that the wrong allegations against jihad can be effectively countered and people do not continue to get swayed by misinterpretations of jihad that would lead them to extremism and impermissible actions, causing harm not only to themselves but also to the worldwide Muslim community or *ummah* in general.

It is thus indispensable for Muslims to have a proper understanding of jihad and its principles and rules. Many of our non-Muslim brethren who sincerely wish for peace and justice are also eager to know what the concept of jihad is all about. I hope that the English translation of my book will meet that need in a modest way.

Both Muslims as well as non-Muslims are victims of misunderstandings about the reality of jihad. The changing times and conditions of the world and the transformation of global affairs have created the urgent need for fresh interpretations of the concept of jihad and for the formulation of new regulations covering its crucial aspects. Many rules governing jihad depend on the prevailing international context and the conditions of human civilization. The views about jihad of many classical Islamic jurists or *fuqaha* and the Muslim Caliphs may have been appropriate for their own particular historical context, but today, when the entire state structure, international relations, and global affairs have undergone tremendous changes, it has become difficult to understand those rules in today's context. I hope this book will be considered a balanced contribution in this regard.

I use the word 'balanced' here because while I uphold and fully respect the *Shari'ah* texts, I have sought to operate within the classical framework of *ijtihad* or creative reflection on the sources of the *Shari'ah* in order to seek to derive Islamic guidelines for today's context. For instance, in the corpus of classical *fiqh* or Muslim jurisprudence, there is simply no concept of permanent peace between Muslim and non-Muslim states. It only mentions short-term peace agreements. It lays down that an Islamic state is permitted to make peace with a non-Muslim state only if the former is weak or is under such compulsion that it simply cannot wage war against the latter. Imam Shafi'i (767–820 CE), for example, argues that an Islamic state cannot make a peace treaty with a non-Muslim state for a period of more than 10 years.

Today, however, we are faced with a very different international situation. What, for instance, is the *Shari'ah* guidance in a situation when Muslims are faced with a non-Muslim state that does not oppress its citizens (including Muslims) or put any hurdles in the path of inviting people to Islam, and allows free and uninhibited practice of Islam in its domains? Can jihad be declared against such a state? To insist that in such a context too jihad must be declared and that such a state must be forced to accept a Muslim government cannot be justified at all. Every community should have the right to be governed by its own people, as long as this government does not engage in persecution and atrocities.

The *Qur'an* (8: 61) itself states that if one's enemy inclines towards peace, Muslims must willingly embrace peace. Then why, one might ask, did the classical *fuqaha* of the early medieval period claim that peace with non-Muslim states was possible only on a temporary basis? This contradiction can easily be resolved if we take into account the historical context which these *fuqaha* were addressing. I have sketched an outline of this context in this book in such a way that the reader might be convinced that while the opinions of the classical *fuqaha* may have been appropriate for their own times, in today's context the situation is different, because of which we need to seek guidance on the matter in the light of the *Qur'an* and the *sunnah*, the practice of the Prophet Muhammad.

Lamentably, some Muslims with only a superficial understanding of the *Qur'an* and the *sunnah* still continue to believe that it is the duty of the worldwide Muslim *ummah* to wage war against the rest of the world. This erroneous belief has been reinforced by the ongoing and relentless imperialist offensives of Western powers and state-sponsored terrorism in other countries, which has forced a section of Muslims to fall prey to extremism and radicalism and to wrong understandings about the Islamic concept of jihad.

Today, in contrast to the times of the classical *fuqaha*, we live in an age where it is possible to conceive of permanent, sustained peace and an international order based on such peace. Further, at least theoretically, no country in the world now places any hurdles in the path of Islamic missionary work or inviting its people to Islam. Because of the astonishing development of the means of communication, we now have new possibilities for Islamic missionary work available to us. This vastly changed context thus leaves no basis, in reason and in the *Shari'ah*, for holding on to the old concept, according to which Muslim states should, as far as possible, avoid entering into peace treaties with other states, and instead, they should wage war against them and thereby seek to bring them under the flag of Islam.

Many Muslim scholars have well understood, and sought to avail of, the possibilities that have been made available in today's vastly changed context, including the now widely-held notion of international peace, in order to invite others to the path of service to, and worship of, God alone. They have sought to redefine discourses about jihad based on their understanding that jihad does not mean snatching the reigns of power from another community or establishing Muslim rule. They rightly point out that as long as possibilities exist for leading one's life according to God's religion and for inviting other people to it, and people are not subjected to imperialist oppression or religious persecution, Muslims must abide by peaceful activism in order to call people to the path of God, revive Islam and to instill within Muslims piety and firm commitment to God so that they lead their lives in accordance with the faith—these are all faces or forms of jihad.

Undoubtedly, if imperialist oppression and religious persecution can only be ended through resort to force, it can constitute jihad—indeed, the best form of jihad—provided that this jihad is waged in accordance with the aims, rules and conditions that God has laid down. Yet, it must also be noted that in the context of today's vastly changed conditions, for this to take a practical form that is in accordance with the spirit of the *Qur'an* and the *sunnah* and that does not violate their explicit texts is extremely difficult. From a believer's viewpoint, it is possible that we may want to empathetically evaluate the position of the classical *fuqaha* when they insist that establishing peace with a non-Muslim state is permissible only if an Islamic state is compelled to do so and has no other choice. At the same time, we should realize the altogether different situation prevailing today. Here we need to possess a proper awareness of the new conditions and context of today as well as a deep understanding of the *Qur'an* and the *sunnah*.

Unfortunately, very limited effort has been made in this regard so far, and that too only superficially and without adducing strong evidence from the *Shari'ah*. Some scholars who have written on the subject have erred, explicitly or otherwise, in the direction of seeking to legitimize Western oppression, past and present. Others have presented a few textual references to back their particular interpretations while ignoring the arguments and references offered by those whose views they critique. Clearly, this is inadequate.

For centuries, the view of the classical *fuqaha* and *ulema* has been carried down, according to which a Muslim state should consider it a duty to wage war, if possible, against non-Muslim states and forcibly incorporate them into its realms. Hence, for any new or different interpretation to be acceptable to many Muslims, it is necessary that it should be presented in such a way that it does not appear to contradict in its entirety the *fiqh* position that had evolved in the past. The classical *fiqh* position should be related to its historical context, and thus it should be shown that it was not a call for unbridled oppression. Lamentably, in my humble opinion, this work has not been done so far.

In this present work, I have tried to explore the possibilities of this approach while at the same time highlighting the rationale behind the position of the classical *fuqaha* about peace with non-Muslim states being simply temporary. I have attempted to locate this position in the particular historical context in which the classical *fuqaha* lived and wrote. Further, I have also sought to explain, by references to the *Qur'an*, that the real aim and underlying basis of Islamic international law is, in fact, peace.

While examining the rules, regulations and principles underlying jihad, it is crucial to bear in mind the social and historical context, processes of civilizational development, and the international scenario. This would help us to appreciate the fact that changed historical contexts demand that the rules of jihad be reformulated in a contextually-sensitive and meaningful manner. Just as with the case of all other *fiqhi* rules, it is possible that when socially accepted customs (*'urf*), the general environment, and the international context change, the detailed regulations about jihad that are based on *ijtihad* might need to change or be reformulated to accord with the demands of justice and wisdom. God has placed this miraculous quality in the *Qur'an* and the practice of the Prophet Muhammad that those who ponder on these sources can gain necessary guidance in terms of principles, from which appropriate rules and laws can be deduced that are based on truth and justice. This book focusses particularly on these basic principles.

Today, Muslims must seriously take up the urgent task of devising such systems and rules in the light of the *Qur'an* and the *sunnah* that confirm Islam's claim that its *Shari'ah* upholds morality, truth and justice in the best possible way. There is no doubt that if the principles of the *Shari'ah* and the texts of the *Qur'an* and *sunnah* are studied properly, it would lead one to the conclusion that international laws and rules of war that these sources outline are indeed based on justice and righteousness.

An important section of this book is devoted to reforming the contemporary extremist ideology regarding jihad. At the same time, I feel it imperative to point out that the emergence and growth of this extremism in recent years owes principally to the enslavement, oppression, and humiliation, whether directly or otherwise, of Muslim countries and peoples and the gross violation of their human rights by America and its allies, as in Iraq and Afghanistan. All of this has resulted in complete denial of justice, which has only further fuelled the flames of Muslim anger. To ignore this is tantamount to turning a blind eye to a grim and undeniable reality. When all means to get justice are denied to an oppressed people, they become psychologically prone to seeking revenge through extremism, although this might actually prove counter-productive for these same people. This extremism cannot be countered unless its actual root causes are seriously addressed.

No book on jihad in our present age can provide a comprehensive picture unless it also discusses the role of international secret service and intelligence agencies in 'jihadist' organizations and acts of terrorism. An increasing number of people today realize that the truth about many 'terrorist' attacks goes much beyond, and sometimes quite contrary to how the media or certain governments present them.

Today, as I mentioned earlier, a huge propaganda offensive is underway at the global level against the Islamic concept of jihad. At the same time, finding all doors to secure justice firmly closed to them and faced with cruel oppression, some Muslims have taken to the path of extremism, which has led them to lose all consciousness of knowledge and wisdom. They have evolved an utterly erroneous interpretation of jihad in the path of God (*jihad fi sabil Allah*), one that is contrary to the *Shari'ah* and does not take into account the rules that the *Shari'ah* sets for jihad and has given a bad name to Islam and to Muslims.

These Muslim extremists may be small in number, but that they do exist cannot be denied. Some of them are undoubtedly being used by international agencies, and have become a major cause for defaming the Islamic concept of jihad and for numerous daunting problems that Muslims now have to contend with. Through their actions, they have provided the greatest excuse to America to meddle in the affairs of Muslim countries, and have afforded certain governments in Muslim countries (which they brand as 'American agents') the pretext to clamp down on Islamic groups and institutions.

Some Muslim intellectuals, under the pressure of adverse conditions and unceasing hostile propaganda, have opted to find fault with their own faith. They have sought to negate the very concept of jihad, or to interpret it in a way that suits the West and its followers. This situation has created great confusion. In this context, there is an urgent need to properly explain the truth about the Islamic concept of jihad. We need to highlight how it is actually based on justice and wisdom, and how those who engage in it, in the manner prescribed by Islam, can indeed be a blessing for all of humankind, Muslims as well as others. This is what this book seeks to do.

With regard to the issue of jihad, it is completely unacceptable that under pressure from the ongoing propaganda against the concept, we should adopt an apologetic or defensive stance. The *Qur'an* instructs us to speak the truth, to announce God's message without fear. I have attempted to do this through this book, by seeking to highlight, in the light of the *Qur'an* and the *sunnah*, the truth about jihad and its principles, rules, regulations and aims, the need for jihad, and the characteristics required of those who engage in it. Keeping these two sources in mind, I have, with God's grace, discussed various sensitive issues related to jihad.

This is not a lengthy tome, but it is the result of considerable study, research and reflection. Appropriate references to quotations taken from the *Qur'an* and the *hadith* have been provided. The *hadith* reports mentioned in the book have been tested carefully by scholars specialized in the field of *hadith* studies, and so may be taken as reliable.

Translating works from Urdu into English on Islamic subjects is not an easy task. For this, the translator requires not just expertise in both languages but also a good understanding of Islamic terminology. It is difficult to find people who combine all three skills. For a while, this difficulty caused me considerable distress, but then I came to know that Dr Yoginder Sikand, who has worked extensively on South Asian Muslim issues, wanted to translate my book. Dr Sikand is a noted scholar, known for his balanced views. I am grateful to him for rendering this book into English.

Finally, I praise and thank God, and pray that He accepts this humble service of mine.

Yahya Nomani

One

The Truth About Jihad

Respect for Human Life

ACCORDING TO the *Qur'an* and the Prophet's *hadith*, the aim of the doctrine of jihad is to promote peace, protection of human life, and freedom. The *Qur'an*, which exhorts its followers to engage in jihad, places great value on the life of a single human being, as indicated in the following verse:

> On that account: We ordained for the Children of Israel that if anyone slew a person, unless it be for murder or for spreading mischief in the land, it would be as if he slew the whole people: and if anyone saved a life it would be as if he saved the life of the whole people. (5:32)

All the legal systems of the world, including the Islamic *Shari'ah*, consider the killing of innocent people as a grievous crime. Islam not only provides legal protection to human life, seeking to prevent killing of innocents by instilling in people fear of the law, but also seeks to develop in their hearts a deep respect for the sanctity of human life. In a *hadith* mentioned in the *Sahih al-Bukhari* (6871), the Prophet is said to have declared killing, along with associating partners with God (*shirk*), as the greatest sin. According to a report in the *Sahih Muslim* (1678), the Prophet reportedly declared that on the Day of Judgment, God will first settle cases of murder.

Islamic teachings about respect for human life apply to every person, Muslim as well as non-Muslim. The Prophet very explicitly stated that if someone slays a non-Muslim whom he is not engaged in an openly declared war with, or who has the protection of a peace agreement with a Muslim government, he would never get to smell the fragrance of paradise (*Sahih al-Bukhari*: 3166).

Permission to Fight

War wreaks destruction. Bloodshed is inevitable in any war. Islam, as indicated above, lays great stress on respect for human life. Therefore, when the *Qur'an* ordains the waging of war, it simultaneously provides adequate reasons for this destructive action.

The *Qur'an* describes war as something bad or destructive, but, like other religions, it does not ignore the fact that, at times, groups, communities, or governments do resort to such terror and oppression that the only way to stop them is through taking up arms. Such brutal oppression of innocent people is a true fact of life, and Islam is a religion of truth and is not blind to reality. It is not like the 'Sermon on the Mount' that insists that if someone hits you on one cheek, you must willingly offer your other cheek for him to slap. Instead, it calls for the hands of oppressors to be restrained, and considers this a way to serve humankind and to gain God's favour.

Islam permits the oppressed, if their lives are under severe threat, to take to arms to protect their life, property and honour. Likewise, it considers it a duty for any country to react in a like manner if it is invaded by another country.

All legal systems in the world agree that it is the right, and even the duty, of every oppressed country or group to suitably reply if attacked. Reason and human conscience are in compliance with this. As the *Qur'an* lays down:

> To those against whom war is made, permission is given (to fight) because they are wronged and verily, Allah is Most powerful for their aid. (22:39)

Further, the *Qur'an* instructs the believers thus:

> Fight in the cause of Allah those who fight you but do not transgress limits; for Allah loveth not transgressors. (2:190)

These teachings are basic to the preservation of the life, respect and freedom of a community, the denial of which would spell death for it, causing it to fall prey to moral decay. Islam aims at character building and the shaping of morals so that people become models of virtue. How, then, can it allow them to sink into degradation by denying them the right to struggle against oppression and persecution? But, it must be remembered, mere fighting in defence against oppression does not constitute legitimate jihad. Rather, jihad must be governed by a host of spiritual and moral principles and laws, observing which alone can qualify it to be truly called 'struggle in God's path' or *jihad fi sabil Allah*.

The biggest misunderstanding about jihad is that it is a communal struggle fought by Muslims, a war that Muslims must launch against other communities to capture power or territory. However, actual facts from the scriptures prove that this sort of war has nothing whatsoever to do with true jihad. The *Qur'an* condemns such violence as *fitna* or spreading 'strife and corruption in the world'. In other words, not every war in which Muslims are involved can be called a jihad. In order for a war to be qualified as a jihad, the *Qur'an* lays down that it must be for only certain purposes and conducted according to specified principles and rules. Any war engaged in by Muslims other than for the purposes laid down in the *Qur'an* or one that violates the rules governing jihad as specified in the *Qur'an* is not a jihad. Rather, it is strife and chaos (*fasad*), which will earn God's wrath.

Aims of Jihad

Jihad for the Sake of Freedom of Religion

The *Qur'an* declared war against the pagans of Mecca in order to end their religious persecution. The Meccans had imprisoned the early Muslims and subjected them to extreme torture and oppression simply because, heeding the voice of their conscience, these people had accepted Islam.

News of their persecution reached the Prophet in Medina. The *Qur'an* then commanded the Muslims thus:

> And fight them on until there is no more persecution and religion to be wholly Allah's. (8:39)

The Arabic word *fitna* is used in the above-mentioned verse with regard to oppression. The verse dictates that the aim of this struggle is to end *fitna*. The term *fitna* actually means 'test' or 'examination', and, according to some noted Arabic scholars, whenever this word or its derivatives are used, it is in the sense of putting something or someone on trial or a test. The term *fitna* has been repeatedly used in the *Qur'an* to describe efforts by the enemies of Islam, in different periods of history, to use force and oppression in an effort to cause Muslims to stray from their faith or to make it difficult for them to remain on the path of Islam. For instance, the *Qur'an* uses a derivate of the word *fitna* in the context of Pharaoh's use of force and oppression to seek to cause those who had accepted the teachings of the Prophet Moses to abandon their faith and return to infidelity:

> But none believed in Moses except some children of Pharaoh's People, through fear of Pharaoh and his chiefs, lest they should persecute them. (10:83)

Elsewhere, the *Qur'an*, using a derivative of the word *fitna*, says:

> Those who persecute (or put into trial) the Believers, men and women and do not turn in repentance (to Allah), will have the Penalty of Hell: they will have the Penalty of the Burning Fire. (85:10)

Some Islamic scholars have interpreted the term to mean shirk or associating partners with God. However, in Arabic, *fitna* does not mean just shirk or shirk without force and oppression. In today's context, *fitna* can be described as 'religious persecution'. Today, the sort of religious persecution that could be called *fitna*, such as the horrendous oppression that the early Muslims faced in Mecca or that those who believed in Prophet Moses had to contend with, is extremely rare.

The duty of Muslims to continue fighting till religious persecution is no more, as laid down in the above-mentioned Qur'anic verse, is echoed in another verse of the *Qur'an*, in the *Surah Al-Baqarah*. Undoubtedly, both these verses relate to the polytheists of Mecca. But, yet, none can deny that seeking to forbid people to follow the religion of their choice by oppressing or even killing them is such a heinous crime that it demands that the defenders of the truth must rise up against this if they have the capacity to do so.

Jihad for the Sake of Freedom of the Oppressed

The *Qur'an* repeatedly refers to the people who engaged in *fitna* in Mecca by seeking to force Muslims to renounce their faith as enemies of God who were persecuting God's hapless servants and threatening their lives. These brutally oppressed Muslims had been crying out for help, appealing for assistance to relieve them of their torment. Finally, God permitted the Muslims of Medina to fight in their defence in the face of the war that had been unleashed on the believers and to protect their lives and faith. They were informed that the conditions had so drastically changed that God's earlier instruction to them to restrain themselves and patiently and steadfastly endure the tortures inflicted on them was no longer necessary. God now commanded them to fight against those Meccan opponents who had declared war on them. As indicated earlier, one of the aims of this war was to put an end to *fitna*, understood here as religious persecution aimed at preventing Muslims from following their faith. As the *Qur'an* says:

> And why should ye not fight in the cause of Allah and of those who, being weak, are ill-treated men, women, and children, whose cry is: "Our Lord! Rescue us from this town, whose people are oppressors; and raise for us from Thee one who will protect; and raise for us from Thee one who will help! (4:75)

With regard to the above-mentioned verse, it can be asked if in the face of the desperate cries of the oppressed for help, a community does not rise up to repel oppression, or is indifferent to the plight of those suffering immense persecution, can it not be said to be totally bereft of basic human feelings? No divine scripture allows for its followers to sit back in comfort while innocent people are being persecuted in this brutal way.

It is true that the oppressed people referred to in the above-mentioned text, who the Muslims were exhorted to help, were their co-religionists. Because of the bond of Islamic brotherhood that they shared with them, these oppressed Muslims had an even greater claim on their help. Yet, this Qur'anic verse, as well as several statements attributed to the Prophet, clearly indicate that it is the duty of a Muslim state to respond to the cries of any wrongfully oppressed community, no matter what its religion, if it has the power to do so, and, for this purpose, to struggle against their oppressors, if need be. People with a proper appreciation of and commitment to Islam need not be reminded that Islam desires that its true followers must rush to the rescue of every wrongfully oppressed person or community, irrespective of religion, without having any ulterior motive. A *hadith* contained in the collection of Abu Daud narrates that the Prophet declared:

'Beware! By God! Keep calling people to the good and preventing them from evil. Catch the hand of the oppressor and force him to ensure justice, and keep striving to bring him to the true path. [In this lies your welfare] otherwise God will cause your hearts to clash with each other's and will curse you, just as He cursed those communities in the past who did not abide by this duty.'

With regard to this sort of jihad that aims at ending oppression, the Prophet very clearly stated, as is evidenced in numerous *hadith* reports, that to make any distinction between the oppressed on grounds of community is against the spirit of Islam. Thus, according to a *hadith* report contained in the *Sunan* of al-Tirmidhi (5167), the Prophet is said to have instructed his followers to help their 'brothers', whether they were oppressed or oppressors. His followers responded, 'We understood the need to help the oppressed, but how should the oppressor be helped?' To this, the Prophet answered, 'Prevent him from oppressing. This is the help that you should give him.'

Two

Not War, But Struggle in the Path of God

WAR FOUGHT in defence and to overcome oppression is a basic human right and duty, but here one point is of extreme significance. After the Prophet shifted to Medina in 622 CE, the town was attacked by the enemies of Islam. That is why God finally sent down revelations ordering the Prophet and his companions to make preparations to defend themselves in the face of these brutal assaults. Yet, at the same time, these verses made it very clear that this defensive war that the Muslims needed to fight was not just for protecting their honour or political freedom. Rather, the *Qur'an* repeatedly stressed that they were not like any ordinary human group that fights for worldly goods and pleasures. Instead, it described them as a people who had turned their faces from the trappings of the world and gathered around the Prophet in order to worship and serve God and to strive for the welfare of the whole of humankind. It depicted them as a group that had vowed to live in poverty, if need be, and to make major sacrifices so that others could also be guided to the straight path. That is why the sort of war that these Muslims were ordered to engage in was not like any war fought for worldly ends. Rather, it was termed as *jihad fi sabil Allah* or 'struggle in the path of God', a war fought for God's sake.

Every community in the world has the right to take up arms to defend itself, in accordance with accepted norms and within acceptable limits. But, the fighting that the Prophet and his followers resorted to was not for political freedom or for the communal rights of Muslims. The early Muslims had become, as it were, the very salt of the earth at a time when there was no community in the world that was wholly and completely based on devotion to, and service of, God. Through not just their words but their actions as well, the Prophet and his followers proved that they had no lust for the luxuries of the world. They adopted poverty for themselves, and took up as their mission the guidance of humankind and the establishment of justice. Caring nothing for worldly comforts, they led a life of service to God and in accordance with His will. So, when they were ordered to fight against those who had launched a reign of terror and oppression against them, they were told by God that this was not simply to defend themselves, but, rather, to defend God's faith on earth. This is why these wars were termed as *jihad fi sabil Allah* and were deemed a source of great divine reward.

The cold hearth of the Prophet's house and the fact that sometimes the Prophet went to sleep without food, with a stone tied round his stomach, are testified to in the history books. Even as Medina's prosperity grew, the Prophet's house remained empty. The Prophet passed away from this world in a state of poverty. His daughter Fatima once approached him and spoke of how her hands had become knotted due to constant use of the grinding stone and how her body was weak. She spoke about how her husband, Ali, was suffering from asthma. She requested the Prophet for financial help. His reply to her was that there were still orphans left in Medina, who had to be helped. Instead of giving her money, he told her to recite *Subhan Allah* ('Glory be to God!'), *Alhamdulillah* ('Praise be to God!') and *Allahu Akbar* ('God is Great!') 33 times every day, explaining that this was more valuable than all the wealth of the world put together.

As I mentioned earlier, the sort of fighting that is regarded as legitimate in Islam has been described in the *Qur'an* as 'struggle in the path of God'. To repeat a point I made before, such fighting cannot be for communal or worldly interests or for the defence of Muslims or for advancing their power and glory. Rather, for a war fought by Muslims to be regarded as a jihad, it must be fought, not just for communal defence or for defending Muslims' lives and properties, but, rather, to gain God's acceptance, to protect His faith, to guide humanity, to promote its welfare, and to save it from oppression and strife. This is why the Prophet explicitly announced that those who fight for their communal interests are not *mujahids*.

Abu Musa al-Ashari, narrated as recorded in the *Sahih* of al-Bukhari (123), a man once appeared before the Prophet and asked him to explain what fighting in the name of God was. He wanted to know if those who fought, driven by anger or communal prejudice, could also be said to be engaged in jihad. The Prophet replied that fighting carried out for the sake of God alone could be said to be a struggle in God's path. This *hadith* report clearly indicates that the aim of a real jihad can never be to acquire worldly wealth or to promote Muslim communal interests.

The aims of jihad that I have outlined above relate to defence in the face of extreme oppression and in order to help save people from such oppression. All legal systems in the world regard this as a reasonable justification for taking up arms. In such a situation, resorting to arms is legitimate, and indeed, sometimes wholly unavoidable. But, from the *Qur'an* and the *hadith* of the Prophet, it is evident that for such a struggle to be called a jihad, it must be that those who participate in it should be so trained, and their hearts should be so purified by following in the path of the prophets of God that they should not be motivated, in any way, by the desire to capture political power for their own community or to enslave another community. Nor should they be driven by the lust for booty or for communal supremacy or by the desire for revenge. Rather, their motive must be to win the pleasure of God, to uphold His faith, to communicate His guidance to humankind, and to help the oppressed.

Unfortunately, in today's age, Muslims have forgotten their mission and the real aims of the jihad. Their general condition does not at all indicate that in God's eyes they have anything to do with the aims and the spirit of jihad that have been mentioned and elaborated upon above. Our condition is now a major cause for our own degradation and for misfortune for the rest of humanity. Today, there is no community that genuinely follows truth and champions justice and that has made service of God its mission, for which it is willing to sacrifice its life and worldly luxuries.

Spirit and Character of *Mujahids*

The *Qur'an* specifies that those oppressed people who were given permission to fight in defence were so faithful and committed to God and the welfare of humanity that if the world were given to them to rule, they would choose to govern in a manner completely different from ordinary rulers. They would use their power and resources for promoting the good and establishing the worship and service of God. Their system of governance would be based on belief in, and fear of, God. They would spend on the poor, and make the promotion of virtue and the prohibiting of vice their guiding principles.

It is in the chapter titled *Al-Hajj* that the *Qur'an* speaks about jihad for the first time. Simultaneously, and in the same context, the *Qur'an* elaborates the necessary characteristics of *mujahids* thus:

> These oppressed people who are being permitted for war are) those who, if We establish them in the land, will establish regular prayer and give regular charity, enjoin the right and forbid wrong. (22:41)

Besides purity of the aims of fighting, proper intention and strict obedience to Islamic rules and *Shari'ah* limits in the conduct of war, this Qur'anic verse also indicates that Muslims who take to the path of jihad and sacrifice must be so committed to God and so morally upright that, if, as a result of their struggle, they gain control of any territory, they would use their power not to satisfy their lusts and base, worldly desires, but, instead, to spread goodness and the service of God and to rid the world of wickedness. Their power would be pressed into the service of God and the welfare of humankind.

On another occasion, the *Qur'an* depicts the spiritual

and moral characteristics of the *mujahids* thus:

> Allah hath purchased of the Believers their persons and their goods; for theirs (in return) is the Garden (of Paradise): they fight in His cause, and slay and are slain: a promise binding on Him in Truth, through the Law [Torah], the Gospel and the *Qur'an*: and who is more faithful to his covenant than Allah? So rejoice in the bargain which ye have concluded: that is the achievement supreme. Those that turn (to Allah) in repentance: that serve Him and praise Him; that wander in devotion to the Cause of Allah; that bow down and prostrate themselves in prayer; that enjoin good and forbid evil; and observe the limits set by Allah; (these do rejoice). So proclaim the glad tidings to the Believers. (9:111–112)

Undoubtedly, jihad undertaken by such a group would be a blessing for humanity, and that is why God rewards such a struggle with great merit. To qualify as a jihad, it must be a struggle for noble aims and engaged in by a group of pure souls to protect humanity from oppression, a step to be taken when all other means have failed.

Offensive Jihad?

I have explained the logic of jihad undertaken in defence and for ending oppression, but the question now arises if offensive war could also, in some cases, be permissible in Islam. Can war be declared against a non-Muslim government that does not in any way oppress Muslims? Can such a government be told either to accept Islam or else hand over power to Muslims, as some people argue?

This is a very crucial question. On the one hand, Islam proclaims itself as the harbinger of justice, and appeals to Muslims not to be lured by the desire for power and wealth for their own sake. How, then, can it call upon Muslims to overthrow and replace with Muslim rule a non-Muslim government that does not engage in any sort of oppression and injustice and that places no hurdle in the path of the Islamic call? It is necessary to study this claim in the light of the basic teachings of the *Shari'ah*.

Some Islamic scholars believe that jihad is permissible in self-defence and for ending *fitna* and oppression, as well as against forces of falsehood that are a hurdle to the spreading of the message and the accomplishment of the mission of the prophets. According to these scholars, after the demise of the Prophet, many of his companions spread out from Arabia into other lands and fought wars for this purpose.

With regard to this issue, it should be kept in mind that the wars fought under the Righteous Caliphs soon after the Prophet's demise against the Persian and Roman Empires were not simply meant to put an end to non-Muslim rule and to establish Islamic rule in their place. In those days, all states were associated with one religion or the other. Every state was strictly identified with a particular religion, and so it was simply inconceivable that any non-Muslim government would allow Muslims to freely invite its subjects to God's path. This is why the issue was never even discussed then of how Muslims should relate to a non-Muslim state that allowed Islam to be practised in its realms or that freely permitted its subjects to accept Islam and follow it.

In the view of a number scholars, in such a situation, Muslims must adopt the path of peacefully inviting others to the faith, making use of this opportunity to the utmost extent possible so much so that all the adequate proofs (*hujjat*) of God are made known. After this, God will Himself decide, in accordance with His practice, which He invariably does after all His proofs have been clearly established. This Divine decision can take any form. My own limited understanding leads me to believe that this opinion is in closer accordance with reason, the spirit of the *Shari'ah*, and the aims and wisdom of God's revelation. This position can be backed by *hadith* reports that insist on the need to peacefully invite people to Islam before fighting can at all be envisaged. And, it must be remembered; today it is no longer forbidden for Muslims to communicate their faith to non-Muslim rulers or to non-Muslims in general.

In support of this argument, one can cite *hadith* reports that insist that before war can be declared against a non-Muslim state, it is incumbent to invite it to the path of Islam. War cannot be considered legitimate without this. In the past, it was felt that if the state authorities refused to accept this invitation, there would be no way to convey the message of Islam to the subjects of that state. Hence, it was thought that such rulers must be removed, through war if necessary, in order that its subjects could hear the call of Islam. And this was a very reasonable position. However, today the situation is completely different. Today, many non-Muslim states pose no restrictions in the path of Islamic *da'wah* or missionary work. Rather, they allow for full opportunities to do so. Given this, it is wrong to say that the mere existence of a non-Muslim government provides enough reason for a Muslim state to wage war against it.

Several Muslims opine that a non-Muslim government would necessarily spread faithlessness, and so God-fearing believers must provide it with only two options: to accept Islam or else to hand over power to them. These Muslims argue that the wars that took place in the early period of Islam against states outside the Arabian Peninsula were fought on the basis of this principle.

A number of scholars have expressed this opinion, and so it needs to be understood with its all conditions. Many of those who hold this view completely ignore, however, some of the very basic and essential conditions of jihad, and so their warped interpretation of jihad becomes unacceptable to non-Muslims as well as many faithful and pious Muslims themselves. I believe that a careful study of the *Qur'an* and the *hadith* reports can supply an adequate answer to this problematic issue.

It must be kept in mind that Islam's teachings about jihad have not been revealed for any community named as 'Muslims'. The basic cause of misunderstanding about jihad stems from conceiving of Muslims as a community like any other, whose main purpose in life is to lead a life of luxury and grandeur. Unfortunately, like others, many Muslims, too, misconceive the notion of the Muslim *ummah* or community in this narrow, communal sense, so much so that this is reflected in the writings of many Islamic scholars. In contrast, as the *Qur'an* conceives it, the Muslim *ummah* is a group of people who are motivated by the desire for felicity in the life after death, by the zeal to serve God and humankind, and by a concern to guide others to God's path, being ready to exert themselves to the utmost for this purpose. It is not a group of people who claim to be Muslims in the formal sense of the term alone.

When this Muslim *ummah* came into being under the leadership of the Prophet Muhammad, it was founded with the following declaration of the *Qur'an*:

> Ye are the best of peoples, evolved for mankind, enjoining what is right, forbidding what is wrong, and believing in Allah. (3:110)

The Muslim *ummah* referred to here was that group that came into being, not on the basis of colour, race, region or land, but, rather, for the purpose of promoting the welfare of the whole of humankind and the service of God. This *ummah* was described in the *Qur'an* as 'the best *ummah*' (*khair-e ummat*) not just because its members had the *Qur'an* in its hands and preached goodness, but also because, as the above-quoted verse indicates, their character was noble and they led the life of those who had truly submitted to God. It was through this nobility of character and purity of faith that they were able to communicate to others the necessary proofs of God and Islam. In other words, this *ummah* of Muslims, who had truly submitted fully to God, rose to the position of a group charged with the mission of upholding the truth and establishing God's proofs and evidences before humankind—or what in the language of the *Shari'ah* is called *itmam-e hujjat*. In such a situation, they were, through their extraordinary character and sacrifice, able to provide people with undeniable evidence of the Truth, leaving them in no doubt about the veracity thereof. This is indicated in the following Qur'anic verse:

> Thus have We made of you an *ummah* justly balanced That ye might be witnesses over the nations and the Messenger a witness over yourselves. (2:143)

In other words, the status of the *ummah* of Muslims, understood here as a group that has sincerely and wholly submitted to God, is that of being witness to the Truth and a symbol of welfare and beneficence. By bearing such witness with regard to God's path, they left no room for differences or doubt. The *Qur'an* explains that this witness of theirs is like that of the Prophet.

Elsewhere, the *Qur'an* repeats the same point:

> It is He Who has named you Muslims, both before and in this [Revelation]; that the Messenger may be a witness for you, and ye be witnesses for mankind! (22:78)

It is the fulfilling of this mission of bearing witness that is the real aim of true jihad. This is why the companions of the Prophet addressed the Persians, saying that they had been sent by God in order to deliver humanity from servitude to other beings and to guide them to serve God instead.

The crux of this argument is that this *ummah* of Muslims that had been formed by the Prophet to guide and reform humankind was willing to make every sacrifice for this purpose. If such a group were told that, if they had the capacity, they should demand from the governments of the world to accept their invitation and thereby be allowed to remain in power, or else, if they opposed them, they should remove them from power so that God's creatures could be served in accordance with His will, would there be anything wrong with this?

The trouble, however, arises from the fact that the Muslims of today are not the same as that pure *ummah* of true believers of the time of the Prophet. Hence, it is wrong for Muslims today, despite not living up to the high standards of faith and piety of the early Muslims, to interpret jihad in such a way as to argue that if a non-Muslim state does not accept Islam, they should declare war against it and replace it with a government of their own. No one can doubt that the Muslims of today do not at all measure up to the standard of being witnesses unto humankind, in contrast the companions of the Prophet. In fact, their condition is so degenerate as to make other people develop negative feelings for Islam. Today's Muslims are almost wholly bereft of true faith in God. In contrast to what Islam teaches, they give greater stress to this world than the world to come after death. In fact, the vast majority of those who call themselves 'Muslims' today lead lives that represent a revolt against God and open disobedience to Him. Further, as far as establishing justice, a welfare system and serving humanity is concerned, which is the basic aim of jihad, many non-Muslim communities are far better than them. It cannot be denied that in causing this sorry decline from what should have been their status, the biggest culprits have been the Muslims themselves. Like other people, they have become slaves of the glitter and glamour of this world. Their general condition is not that of a community inspired by service to God and the desire for success in the Hereafter. In fact, as regards morals, we Muslims are much worse off than many other communities.

In such a situation, who can indeed accept the claim that if the reigns of power were taken away from others and given to the Muslims, the latter would put an end to strife, oppression, conflict, tumult and corruption, and replace them with genuine human welfare and goodness? In fact, if others think that all our talk about disinterested service of humanity and sincere obedience to God is nothing but verbal falsehood, we must accept that our collective hypocritical character alone is responsible for this. Of course, no share of the blame for this accrues to Islam itself. Glance at the general character of Muslims today, at their countries and societies, and think if anyone will at all believe that Muslims actually want to fight other communities in order to end all the evils on earth and replace it with welfare for all! The answer is a resounding 'No'. In such a situation, this sort of interpretation of jihad clearly reflects a very superficial understanding of Islam, a very dangerous violation of the limits set by the *Shari'ah*. Lamentably, in the recent past, several Muslim thinkers and leaders of Muslim movements have widely propagated this wrong interpretation of jihad, and some continue to do so today.

Those who have studied the *Qur'an* and the Prophet's teachings know well that according to the laws of God, whenever Muslims betray their role of being witnesses to the truth, stray from the path of Islam, and earn God's anger, they cannot acquire the sort of power or honour needed to successfully launch any offensive war. In a situation like this, the Muslims would be unable to defend even their own territories and freedoms.

Jihad and Imperialism

The jihad that Islam permits, as has been mentioned earlier, is only for certain purposes. It must abide by certain rules and conditions. It must be inspired solely by the desire for closeness to God and by indifference to worldly pleasures and luxuries. Such a jihad is a need and, indeed, a blessing for humankind in order to end the darkness of oppression and evil. At the same time, it is possible that some Muslim groups who claim to be engaged in jihad are bereft of the character required of true *mujahids*. Yet, this does not mean that the Islamic doctrine of jihad itself is faulty.

Every thinking person will agree with this assertion of the *Qur'an* that if the spirit of jihad and people inspired by it were emptied from the world, it would mean the victory of evil:

> And had God not repelled people some by others, there had been demolished monasteries, churches, synagogues and mosques, wherein God's Name is mentioned much. (22:40)

The *Qur'an* says that in the absence of resisting oppression in this manner, there would be nothing to stop the evil of strife and bloodshed in the world. In other words, it is a major blessing from God that through his prophets, He has ordered His chosen slaves to purify themselves of greed for power and wealth, to struggle to extirpate strife and oppression from the world, and to guide humankind and work for its welfare, using, if need be, violence in the form of jihad for this purpose.

Today, we are faced with a strange situation. Prior to the present 'Age of Culture and Civilization' heralded by the West, kingdoms would wage war against each other for land, resources, and imperial glory. This was considered one of the main objectives of states in those days. Naturally, their conduct of war and their behaviour towards the people of the territories they conquered were shaped by that objective. These states never claimed to be champions of peace, tolerance and harmony. Nor did they claim to be promoting democracy, respect for human rights and cultural enlightenment through the wars that they waged. Rather, their objective in engaging in war was very clear. In contrast, today powerful Western governments, impelled by imperialistic and hegemonic designs, wage ruthless wars, albeit in the name of 'peace'. They claim that the wars they launch are for the sake of 'civilization', 'human welfare and positive development', and protecting 'human rights' and 'democracy'. These Western powers have created new records in contradicting words by deeds. They shed the blood of thousands of innocent people while parroting slogans of 'democracy' and 'equality'. This new situation has caused many people to doubt if the claims that Islam also makes about global progress and welfare are not also just empty slogans, and that, in actual fact, it aims simply at seizing power.

It is not right to judge a doctrine or ideology by the

acts and practices of those who claim to be its adherents. As a religion and ideology, Islam is a spiritual message and invitation. Its real aim is not to capture power for a particular community or to ensure that a particular community should rule. Rather, its aim is to promote the moral values and spiritual truths that form the basis of its message. If Muslim political power helps to promote this aim, it is desirable. However, if it proves to be a hurdle in the path of this goal, it is hateful, and the *Qur'an* indicates that God will certainly destroy such power of the Muslims and make them face utter humiliation. Islam has blessed jihad as a struggle in God's path. Those who engage in jihad must forever be mindful of the Day of Judgment, when each soul will have to stand before God and account for its deeds. For, as the *Qur'an* says:

> That House of the Hereafter We shall give to those who intend not high-handedness or mischief on earth: and the End is (best) for the righteous. (28:83)

If, as a consequence of jihad, God grants His slaves the opportunity to govern, they must realize that this is a custody for which they will be accountable to God. If someone misuses this opportunity and, instead of regarding it as custody from God, uses it to acquire worldly honour, power and luxury, he will be severely punished on the Day of Judgment. When God appointed the Prophet David as a ruler, He instructed him thus:

> O David! We did indeed make thee a vicegerent on earth: so judge thou between men in truth (and justice): nor follow thou the lusts (of thy heart), for they will mislead thee from the Path of Allah: for those who wander astray from the Path of Allah, is a Penalty Grievous, for that they forget the Day of Account. (38:26)

Being constantly mindful of the Day of Judgment alone can safeguard this custody in the hands of rulers so that, despite having vast powers, they do not transgress the limits set by God. In a *hadith* report recorded in the *Sahih Muslim*, the Prophet once instructed his companion Abudhar regarding the grave responsibilities concerning the great custody that governance is, adding that on the Day of Judgment it would cause rulers to suffer, save for those who ruled according to the truth and abided by their responsibilities (*Sahih Muslim*: 1826).

We have briefly outlined the regulations that Islam has laid down in order to keep jihad in the path of God within the moral limits set by God. The finest practical model of jihad was provided by the Prophet Muhammad. Orientalist scholars have sought to explain the jihads of the Prophet in terms of the economic marginalization of the Arabs of that time, especially the Bedouins. They claim that the real intention of jihad in Islam was to acquire wealth. This is not true at all. If this were really the case, why would the leaders of these jihads themselves, the Prophet Muhammad, and Abu Bakr and Umar, the first two caliphs, have remained poor till they departed from this world? By the time the Prophet expired, the whole of Arabia had been conquered. Wealth had come into Medina, and had also been distributed to the poor, but, yet, food was still cooked only once a day in the Prophet's house (*Sahih Muslim*: 2974). At the time he departed from this world, this was made possible only through borrowing money from a Jew (*Sahih al-Bukhari*: 2916).

In the Prophet's time, the largest war booty was secured in the aftermath of the war of Hawazin. The people of Hawazin had brought along all their wealth with them to the battlefield. When they were defeated, their wealth fell into the hands of the Muslims. If the aim of this or the other jihads of the Prophet's time was lust for wealth, this booty from Hawazin would surely have been sent to the homes of the Muslims of Medina. Instead of that, however, the Prophet distributed all the wealth among the Quraish and to the chiefs of some other tribes who, till recently, had been leaders of the enemies of the Muslims. The pious, faithful Ansars, or Muslims of Medina, got nothing of this at all. Consequently, some Ansars were upset. Hearing about this, the Prophet called the Ansars and instructed them, saying, 'Won't you be happy that the people take the worldly things and you take Allah's Apostle to your homes, reserving him for yourself?' They replied in the affirmative.

Syria, an immensely fertile land, was conquered during the rule of the Caliph Umar (d 644 CE). As mentioned in the book *Futuh al-Buldan*, in many places the Syrians actually welcomed the Muslim forces. The Muslims had to face confrontations mainly in those cities where the Byzantine army had encampments. The Syrians were mainly Christians, followers of the same faith as their Byzantine rulers, but yet they welcomed the Muslims as liberators. On account of certain military compulsions, it so happened that the Muslims had to withdraw from Homs, Damascus and Baalbek. As they were doing so, the Christians of these towns appealed to them not to depart, pleading with them not to leave them at the mercy of the cruel Byzantine soldiers. When the Muslims explained to them why they had to leave, the Syrian Christians prayed to God for the Muslims to return. They promised the Muslims that if the Byzantine army invaded their cities, they would join hands with the Muslims in order to fight them.

As this event illustrates, true jihad is not based on lust for power and wealth, but, rather, is for the sake of God and concern for human welfare and justice. The Prophet's jihads very clearly illustrate that true jihad has nothing at all to do with imperialism or lust for power. Rather, it aims to destroy such imperialism.

Three

Reconciliation and Jihad

THE BASIC law underlying inter-community relations in Islam is reconciliation (*sulh*). That is to say, the relations that a Muslim state should ideally enjoy with other states in the world should be based on peaceful reconciliation.

When the *Qur'an* gives Muslims permission to fight, it also mentions, with regard to the justification of fighting, that this is permitted to those who have been made the target of war or oppression by others. The Meccan oppressors had made it exceedingly difficult for those who wanted to follow God's path on their own free will. They so badly tormented the Muslims of Mecca that many of them had to flee the town. Even after the Prophet and many of his companions had settled in Medina, their Meccan opponents did not cease their relentless, violent attacks. This is why God permitted the Muslims to fight back, so that this religious persecution or *fitna* could be put an end to. As the *Qur'an* points out:

> Persecution (*fitna*) is worse than slaughter. (2:217)

In the same Qur'anic verse, when Muslims were for the first time instructed to take to fighting, God addressed them thus:

> Fight in the cause of Allah those who fight you but do not transgress limits; for Allah loveth not transgressors. And slay them wherever ye catch them, and turn them out from where they have turned you out; for the persecution and oppression are worse than slaughter. (2:190–191)

These verses indicate that the wars fought by the Prophet aimed to put an end to religious persecution and harsh oppression. From these Qur'anic verses, it very clearly emerges that Islam regards war as essentially something bad or negative. With regard to the *Qur'an*'s declaration that persecution and oppression are worse than slaughter (2:217), the noted scholar Ibn Taimiyah (1263–1328 CE) writes, 'This verse implies that although war entails strife and conflict, yet the strife and conflict caused by persecution (*fitna*) by the disbelievers is even more terrible than that' (*Majma-ul Fatawa*: 28/355).

This is why the *Qur'an* regards war as something that requires to be justified morally by adequate reasons. The *Qur'an* specifies that *fitna* is worse than slaughter. Hence, it considers that war might, in certain circumstances, become essential for eliminating *fitna*. This is why, following the Battle of Badr in 624 CE, the *Qur'an* ordered the Muslims to fight the pagans of Mecca in order to end their religious persecution and oppression and to remove the hurdles that the Meccans had put in the path of inviting people to Islam. The *Qur'an* instructed the Muslims to fight against them so that *fitna* was ended and worship remained for God alone. Here the *Qur'an* goes further in exhorting Muslims to wage war and declares:

> Against them make ready your strength to the utmost of your power, including steeds of war, to strike terror into (the hearts of) the enemies of Allah and your enemies and others besides whom ye may not know but whom Allah doth know. (8:60)

After this, the *Qur'an* exhorted the Muslims to spend their wealth in making preparations for war and to be prepared for sacrificing their lives. Yet, at the same time as it inspired them to take to the battlefield it also proclaimed:

> But if the enemy incline towards peace, do thou (also) incline towards peace, and trust in Allah: for He is the one that heareth and knoweth (all things). Should they intend to deceive thee—verily Allah sufficeth thee. (8:61–62)

The particular background and specific context of the revelation of the above-quoted verse need to be noted. The verses just before this one exhorted the believers to make preparations to wage war against their oppressors, but in this verse, God told them that they must accept peace if their enemy inclined towards it. Now, it could be possible that doubts could arise as to the intention of the enemy in suing for peace, for the enemy might use this as a stratagem to deceive. In response, this verse says that Muslims should incline towards peace and place total trust in God, adding that this trust alone is the true support for the believers. In other words, it cautions Muslims not to unnecessarily doubt and worry about the possibility of treachery by the enemy.

These verses of the *Qur'an* were revealed with regard to the pagans of Mecca, whom the Muslims were then at war with. They were stiff opponents of Islam. They had conspired to extirpate Islam and destroy its citadel, Medina. The Jewish tribes were hand-in-glove with the Meccan pagans in this. The actual aim of these verses was to exhort Muslims to go to war, but yet, in the same context, the *Qur'an* advised Muslims that if their enemies inclined towards peace, they must do the same, and place their trust in God, although their enemies were untrustworthy and that it was possible that the latter could renege on their promises and betray them.

On the basis of these verses, we can say that it is wrong to suppose that peace between Muslims and others is conceivable only when the Muslims' position is so weak that they are unable to wage war. The background of these Qur'anic verses that speak about the need to accept offers of peace indicates that the Muslims' position at that time was certainly not weak. In fact, the verses exhort Muslims to fight. One of these verses even declares:

> O Prophet! Rouse the Believers to the fight. If there are twenty amongst you, patient and persevering, they will vanquish two hundred: if a hundred, they will vanquish a thousand of the Unbelievers: for these are a people without understanding. (8:65)

It must be remembered that these verses were revealed after the grand victory of the Muslims at the Battle of Badr.

So, if at such a time the Muslims were ordered to accept the offer of peace made by a fierce enemy, it obviously indicates that it is wrong to believe that peace can only be accepted when Muslims are weak and that it should not when Muslims are in a strong position. This argument is completely fallacious, because at the time the above-quoted verse was revealed, the Muslims were not under any compulsion. Furthermore, it cannot be said with regard to the peace treaty that the Prophet entered into with the Meccans in the sixth year of the Islamic calendar that at that time too Muslims were in a weak position. In fact, the Muslims had vanquished the Meccans several times before that.

Peace is Temporary in the Corpus of *Fiqh*

The above-mentioned verses clearly indicate that when the possibilities for peace exist, Islam teaches that peace must be accepted. Yet, at the same time, the corpus of *Fiqh* developed by Muslim scholars after the Prophet does not, in general, reflect this understanding that the basic principle of Islam underlying inter-community relations is peace. Instead, the books of *fiqh* create the impression that peace is something to be accepted by Muslims only as a temporary measure and only when it is deemed absolutely necessary.

The reason for this must be located in the particular historical context when the corpus of *fiqh* came to be developed, including the then prevailing level of human civilization and the inter-communal and political situation. These *fiqh* rules were seen as the *Shari'ah* prescriptions for that age. It must be remembered that at that time, the concept of permanent peace simply did not exist anywhere in the world. In both practical as well as ideological terms, the notion of such peace was completely foreign for governments and states in that age. The state of human civilization at that time was such that if any state found it possible or feasible to declare war and capture the territory of another state, it considered its duty to do so.

There was another crucial aspect of the then prevailing system of inter-community relations because of which the *ulema* felt it their duty to warn Muslim rulers to accept peace only when compelled to do so. This had to do with the fact that, in those days, each state was closely allied to, and identified with, one or another religion. In fact, every government was based on some or the other religious ideology. Naturally, in that age it was simply inconceivable that any non-Muslim government would open the doors to Muslims to freely call their subjects to God's path. In this way, they became a major hurdle between God and His slaves, preventing the latter from hearing and accepting God's message. In such a context, accepting peace as the permanent norm would naturally have meant that Muslims would have had to abstain from their duty of calling others to God's path and His service. Obviously, it was impossible for the Muslim *ummah* to accept this on a permanent basis, for it would have gone completely against the basic role and duty of the *ummah*. This is why the *ulema* and scholars of fiqh of those times expressed the view that Muslim states should accept peace with non-Muslim states only on a temporary basis and simply out of pragmatism and the compulsion of circumstance.

The *Qur'an*'s insistence that war can be declared to overcome the *fitna* of the forces of falsehood that use force to damage or block the mission of the prophets of God and that are a barrier between God and His slaves is undoubtedly correct. Other than for this, however, it must be noted, according to Islam, peace remains the basic principle underlying inter-community relations.

Some people claim that the above-quoted Qur'anic verse that speaks of making peace with enemies was later abrogated, and that it was replaced by other verses that were revealed after it that command Muslims to wage war against the polytheists. Most Qur'anic commentators do not agree with this claim, however. For instance, with regard to this verse, the noted Islamic scholar Ibn Jarir Tabari (d 923 CE) writes:

"If they [the enemies] agree with you [Muslims] to stop fighting and accept peace, and, irrespective of whether they accept Islam or pay the *jizya* or reconcile or establish peace in any other way, you, too, should incline towards peace and do what they want and give what they want."

With regard to those who claim that the verses commanding acceptance of offers of peace have been abrogated, Ibn Jarir Tabari adds:

"No proof of this [claim] can be advanced from the *Qur'an* or the *sunnah* or from reason (*'aql*) or nature (*fitrah*)."

If facts be looked at, the two different types of Qur'anic verses—exhorting Muslims to fight and ordering them to make peace—were revealed for different conditions and circumstances. The verses that talk of peace relate to a situation wherein the opponent wishes to cease fighting and accept peace. On the other hand, the verses that exhort Muslims to fight relate to a context where their opponents have unleashed a full-fledged war against the Muslims. In that situation, for Muslims to sit back and not take any suitable action would be tantamount to weakness and accepting degradation. That is why this was forbidden, and the *Qur'an* declared:

> Be not weary and faint-hearted, crying for peace. And ye should be Uppermost: for Allah is with you. (47:35)

Important Clarification

In the above-mentioned verses, Muslims were exhorted to fight the Meccan pagans so that *fitna* and religious persecution were put an end to and religion would be for God alone. I have already explained what is meant by the term *fitna*. To repeat, it means to harass, to oppress and to compel someone through force, persecution and coercion. Those commentators who have wrongly interpreted *fitna* to mean simple *shirk* or polytheism have done so because once a series of wars had broken out between the Muslims and the pagan Arabs, the Muslims were ordered to continue fighting until the very roots of polytheism were uprooted from Arabia. In actual fact, however, to repeat a point that I just made, *fitna* does not mean polytheism alone.

A major clarification needs to be made here. This relates to the point made in the *Qur'an* that war should continue till religion is for God alone. This certainly does not mean that non-Muslims must be forced, through war, to accept Islam. The fact that the *Qur'an* allows Muslims to take *jizya* from non-Muslims and enter into a peace treaty to protect them clearly suggests that non-Muslims are not to be forced to accept Islam. Further, it also does not mean that the concept of jihad is based on the notion that only Muslims and no other community has the right to establish an independent government. In actual fact, this order applies only to the Arabian Peninsula, where Muslims are told not to allow any government but one based on Islam to exist. The status of Mecca was like an Abrahamic and Ishmaelite endowment, being associated with the Prophet Abraham and his son Ishmael, and so the entire land inhabited by the descendants of Ishmael, the Arabs, was to be reserved for Islam, the religion of Abraham, so that it could become the global centre for the Abrahamic call to faith. Accordingly, the final objective of the series of wars in the Arabian Peninsula at the time of the Prophet was to make the whole of that territory come under the religion of God.

This is precisely why the Prophet Muhammad willed that pagans, Jews and Christians be removed from the Arabian Peninsula (*Sahih al-Bukhari*: 3035; *Sahih Muslim*: 1767). This is also why the Prophet announced that there was no space for any religion other than Islam in the Arabian Peninsula (*Mu'wata*: 1388). This rule, it is crucial to note, applied only to the Arabian Peninsula, while other religions were allowed to exist outside this region. This is the unanimous opinion of Muslim scholars.

From this detailed discussion, it clearly emerges that if any non-Muslim community sincerely wants to establish peace with Muslims, its offer must be accepted. This also means that if any non-Muslim state agrees to be at peace with Muslims, and allows for the peaceful practice and propagation of Islam in its territories and does not engage in any force or *fitna* in this regard, Muslims must accept its offer and use peaceful methods to invite others to the faith so much so that the 'proofs' (*hujjat*) of God are established. After this, in accordance with His established ways, God will open a way.

If something leads to distance from God
It causes knowledge to be *fitna*,
Children, wealth and lands to be *fitna*,
The sword that is wielded for the
oppressed to be *fitna*,
And not just the sword, but even the call
'God is the Greatest!' to be *fitna*.

Four

Important Conditions and Rules Regarding Jihad

Obedience of Imam

WAR INVOLVES terrible bloodshed and destruction. That is why any minor deviation from the proper rules of warfare can convert a jihad in the path of God into tumult, strife and chaos. It was because of this that the Prophet very clearly and explicitly laid down that if a Muslim government exists, all decisions relating to jihad must be made by it alone. Disobeying the decisions of the Muslim government in this regard is not at all permissible. There are clear instructions relating to this in the *Qur'an* and the *hadith*.

In the corpus of *fiqh* developed by the early *ulema*, there is not even the slightest hint of people declaring jihad without the permission of their rulers. As the famous *fiqh* text *Kitab al-Mughni* clearly states, "The matter of jihad depends on the decision of the Muslim ruler." It is thus clear that where there exists a government of the Muslims, jihad can be conducted only under its banner. Citizens of that state cannot engage in jihad independently of the state or without its permission. It cannot be that their state has a peace treaty with another country and, despite this, they declare jihad against that country. This they might only do if they renounce their citizenship and do not become citizens of any regular state, or if they set up a state of their own, in which case they can take decisions for themselves.

However, till they remain citizens of a state and either reside there or in some other country while being citizens of such a state, they do not have the right to make decisions about war and peace on their own. Under all circumstances, they will have to abide by the treaties with other states entered into by the state of which they are citizens. This is an explicit commandment of God and the Prophet Muhammad. The importance of this commandment does not in any way diminish if anyone defies or ignores it.

Hence, if some emotionally-driven Muslims become

a threat to the life and property of the citizens of a non-Muslim state that has diplomatic relations and peace treaties with the state of which these Muslims are citizens, it is a gross violation of the *Shari'ah*, irrespective of how noble the intention of such Muslims may be.

In this context, it can be said that, in the recent past, in the wake of despicable incidents of traducing the Prophet Muhammad, the Muslims who issued appeals for the murder of those behind these incidents, or those Muslims who praised such killings clearly ignored the principles of the *Shari'ah*. As long as the government of the country whose citizens are a group of Muslims, has a peace agreement with another government, it is not at all permissible for these Muslims to harm any citizen of the latter country, no matter what complaint they might have against that country. There is only one way for that to happen, and that is if one's country snaps all relations and agreements with the other country.

In the same way, Muslims who are citizens of a non-Muslim state, or who have adopted the citizenship of such a state have, in effect, entered into an agreement to become part of that state. By accepting common citizenship with the other citizens of that state, they must accept and agree to relate with peace with, and to protect the lives and properties of all the citizens of that state. If the non-Muslim state of which they are citizens attacks a Muslim state, they should, on the basis of their rights as citizens, seek to dissuade their state from carrying on fighting, but they cannot take up arms against their state. That they can only do if they renounce their citizenship and openly declare that they have ended what is, in effect, their treaty with that state. Islam has clearly forbidden Muslims from causing damage to ordinary non-combatant civilians even in times of war. After entering into an agreement of common citizenship with non-Muslims in a particular state, this rule leaves no room at all for Muslims to engage in any such destructive acts.

Today, in the face of the sufferings and cruel killings of Muslims in many parts of the world, a large number of Muslim youths are extremely disturbed and angry. They want to stand up to make sacrifices for their co-religionists. This feeling is understandable, and, indeed, praise-worthy, but only if it is given proper direction and used in accordance with *Shari'ah* principles can it prove to be a major force for the reconstruction of the Muslim *ummah*. Two basic aims of the *Shari'ah* which God wants us to observe are upholding the honour of Islam and promotion of goodness in the world. If we violate the *Shari'ah*, neither can we achieve these objectives and nor can we be worthy of receiving God's help. And, we must constantly remember, the *Shari'ah* has made it incumbent on Muslims to abide by the treaties they enter into.

With regard to practical jihad efforts, over the last two decades or more, several Muslim groups in different countries have made serious errors. Unfortunately, we did not notice, or else ignored, the excesses and wrongs committed by them. But, now, witnessing the results of the inner working of what can be called the 'jihadist phenomenon' that are now coming to light, we realize these faults. One of their greatest mistakes was to establish jihadist groups independent of existing Muslim governments.

The Western powers who, in the wake of the Soviet invasion of Afghanistan, helped such jihadist organizations were not in the least concerned that once they had achieved their ends, huge problems would emerge. This was because the damage that would ensue would, or so they believed, be limited simply to the Muslim countries of Asia and their immediate neighbours. Unfortunately, even the rulers and elites of Muslim countries were not at all concerned about this. Moreover, the religious figures who led and supported these jihadist groups in countries such as Egypt, Yemen, Saudi Arabia and Pakistan, did not bother about the implications of these groups and their activities for the future. Nor did they care about the immense threat involved in their countries' taking the help of dangerous and criminal international agencies and allowing them to interfere with local jihadist groups and movements. They also did not consider if it was at all wise, and in accordance with the *Shari'ah*, to arm various independent armed groups to wage war.

Important Practice of the Prophets

Until the Muslims had established a regular government in Medina, the Prophet did not receive any instruction from God to engage in armed jihad. It was only after the Muslims shifted to Medina and established a state under the Prophet that the Muslims were ordered to take to this sort of jihad. This jihad was kept entirely under the supervision of a regular state and government. The history prior to the Prophet Muhammad also indicates that true believers in God engaged in warfare only after an established government had come into being. This is well brought out in the case of the 'Children of Israel' as mentioned in the *Qur'an*.

At the time of Moses and his brother Aaron, the ruler of Egypt subjected the Children of Israel to terrible torture and oppression. Yet, they did not resort to war. Later, they migrated out of Egypt and, in this way, the Children of Israel formed an independent community under an established leadership of their own. Only after that were they ordered by God to engage in jihad.

After this, when the Children of Israel suffered a terrible decline and were subjugated by others, they had to flee from their lands and were widely dispersed, as a result of which their communitarian solidarity was destroyed. The *Qur'an* relates that at this time, some leaders of the community approached their prophet (Samuel) in order to suggest that they should launch a war against their enemies. They requested him to issue instructions to make arrangements for this jihad. They asked him to appoint a head, an established ruler over them, under whose leadership they could engage in jihad and thereby free their lands. The *Qur'an* relates that initially Samuel was reluctant to do this. But later, a jihad was launched, under his command, and, with God's help, the enemy was defeated (2:246–253).

This does not mean that if any non-Muslim power attacks and oppresses a Muslim state and topples its government, Muslim citizens are exempted from engaging in jihad against it. After all, the *Shari'ah* exists to protect Islam, not to destroy it. For, as the *ulema* stress, if in a certain place there is no government at all, Muslims must not, if the need so arises, delay in engaging in jihad because otherwise the very objective of jihad would be defeated. This means that if an oppressive power invades a Muslim country and displaces its government, the inhabitants of that country must defend their lives, property and country despite the absence of an established regular Muslim government.

In places where there is no established government, people are free to make their own choices. There is an instance of this from the time of the Prophet Muhammad. Some Muslims of Mecca were brutally oppressed by the Meccan pagans but had no opportunity to flee the town. According to the terms of the Treaty of Hudaibiyah that the Meccan pagans had entered into with the Prophet Muhammad in 628 CE, if any Muslim left Mecca for Medina, he would have to be returned to Mecca.

It so happened that a hapless Muslim named Abu Basir fled to Medina, and two men came from Mecca to bring him back. Abiding by the terms of the treaty, the Prophet allowed him to be taken back to Mecca. On the way back, Abu Basir killed one of the men, and the other man escaped. Thereafter, Abu Basir got together with some other people and set up camp in an uninhabited place outside the limits of the Muslim state of Medina. Soon these men began attacking trade convoys belonging to the Meccan pagans. The responsibility for this could not be placed on the Prophet or the Medinese state because this group was outside the jurisdiction of Medina (*Sahih al-Bukhari*: 2731).

In this context, it is pertinent to note that some writers have sought to argue that war fought in defence by Muslims in Afghanistan and Iraq against American aggression is not in accordance with the *Shari'ah* on the grounds that such war can be waged only by an established state. They claim that popular resistance in the absence of an established state is tantamount to 'terrorism'. This is an absurdly wrong position. The fact that the Prophet did not forbid Abu Basir from taking up arms is an adequate reply to their specious argument. If his action was wrong, then surely the Prophet would have prohibited it.

Five

Jihad and Abiding by Treaties

ISLAM INSISTS that Muslims should abide by the pacts and treaties that they enter into with others. The *Qur'an* repeatedly insists on this. In one place, it says:

> [A]nd keep the covenant. Lo! Of the covenant it will be asked. (17:34)

The Prophet once remarked, "He who is untrustworthy lacks faith, and he who breaks his agreements has no religion" (*Al-Musnad*: 1668).

From the *Qur'an* and the *sunnah* of the Prophet, it emerges that a treaty between two states or between an individual and a state to ensure peace and security of life and property deserves to be respected. This insistence on abiding by pacts entered into with others is a central Islamic teaching, and those who break their treaties are warned of punishment in Hell. The Islamic doctrine of jihad in the path of God must be understood in this light. The Prophet Muhammad remarked:

"On the Day of Judgment, when all of humankind shall assemble before God, every oath-breaker shall be given in his hand a flag [...] on which shall be written that he, son of his father, is a traitor" (*Sahih al-Bukhari*: 6177; *Sahih Muslim*: 1735).

The aim of war in Islam is not simply to secure victory on the battlefield. Muslims are meant to be upholders of certain moral values even while fighting. If, in the course of fighting, they forget or abandon those values, they shall be irreparably deprived. How will they then be able to engage in inviting others to the path of the faith? How will they then be in a position to establish the 'proofs' of God and His faith before others? The aim of armed jihad in Islam is to guide human beings to God's path and communicate the message of Islam to them through kindness. A true *mujahid* seeks to invite people to save themselves from punishment in the life after death and to call them to the path of blessing and success in this world and in the next. How, then, can he allow himself to be blemished by being misused? How can those who engage in jihad for such a great task consider themselves to be above or beyond moral and ethical restraints? A true jihad is one which, at all costs, preserves, displays and expresses proof of its moral worth before the world. If Muslims wage war for their personal victory or for the sake of their own community, and engage in unethical acts in the course of this, theirs can by no means be considered a jihad, fought for, and in the path of, God.

On the other hand, those who, if the need arises, take up arms for the sake of God's faith, and whose aim is to sacrifice themselves for God, can never deviate from the moral path. Nor can they break their oaths even while engaged in fighting. This is the glory of jihad fought in the way of God. This is why it is incumbent upon Muslims that even if they perceive personal or communal benefit in reneging on their treaties or personal or communal damage in abiding by them, they must faithfully abide by the agreements that they have made with others.

Islam Demands Abiding by Pacts, not Betrayal

In the context of its teachings about war, the *Qur'an* repeatedly points to the need for Muslims to abide by the treaties that they have entered into. The polytheists of Mecca were the most inveterate enemies of the Muslims. They sought to cause the greatest possible damage to the Prophet and his companions. Yet, the *Qur'an* insisted that the Prophet and his followers must abide by the treaties that they had entered into with them. The *Surah At-Tawbah* of the *Qur'an* announced grievous Divine punishment for the Meccan polytheists, and called upon Muslims to issue them an ultimatum of just four months to either accept Islam or else, because of the special position of the Arabian Peninsula, to be cleared off from that territory. After that four month period was over, it laid down that Muslims would be free to attack them. The reason for this was that the Meccan polytheists had continued to oppress Muslims and had violated the agreements that they had entered into with them. In this announcement of war against them, the *Qur'an* ordered the Muslims thus:

> But when the forbidden months are past, then fight and slay the Pagans wherever ye find them, and seize them, beleaguer them, and lie in wait for them in every stratagem (of war). (9:5)

After this, it advised that despite the continued oppression and enmity of the polytheists, Muslims must abide by their treaties if those they had entered into agreements with still abided by them. Thus, the *Qur'an* declared:

> (But the treaties are) not dissolved with those Pagans with whom ye have entered into alliance and who have not subsequently failed you in aught, nor aided any one against you. So fulfill your engagements with them to the end of their term: for Allah loveth the righteous. (9:4)

Further, it added:

> How can there be a league before Allah and His Messenger, with the pagans, except those with whom ye made a treaty near the Sacred Mosque? As long as these stand true to you stand ye true to them: for Allah doth love the righteous. (9:7)

The basic point that these verses make is that Muslims should take a tough stance against those polytheists whose hearts were aflame with hatred of Islam and who wished to annihilate the Muslims. These polytheists did not care for the agreements that they had entered into with the Muslims. Naturally, there could be no agreement with such people. The *Qur'an* elaborated on this as follows:

> How (can there be such a league), seeing that if they get an advantage over you, they respect not in you the ties either of kinship or of covenant? With (fair words from) their mouths they entice you, but their hearts are averse to you; and most of them are rebellious and wicked. The signs of Allah have they

> sold for a miserable price, and (many) have they hindered from His way: evil indeed are the deeds they have done. In a Believer they respect not the ties either of kinship or of covenant! It is they who have transgressed all bounds. (9:8–10)

The *Qur'an* here exhorted Muslims to wage war, but even in such extreme circumstances, when Muslims were faced with inveterate and evil enemies, it added, with regard to 'those with whom you made a treaty near the Sacred Mosque, that if they honor and uphold such a treaty, you shall uphold it as well. God loves the righteous' (9:7). This indicates that if Muslims renege on their agreements, in such cases they would not be considered to be among the righteous nor deserving of God's love.

The Prophet exemplified the principles of jihad in his own personal life and showed us that even during war one must abide by agreements with others. The number of Meccan fighters at the Battle of Badr was around three times that of the Muslims. The Muslims were thus greatly outnumbered. At this time, Huzaifa Ibn Yaman and his father set out to join the Muslim army but fell into the hands of the Meccan polytheists. The Meccans released them on the condition that they would not fight alongside the Muslims. The two men then headed for Badr, where they related what had befallen them to the Prophet. The Prophet instructed them thus: "Return. We shall abide by agreements and shall ask God for assistance" (*Sahih Muslim*: 1787).

If a Muslim government has entered into a treaty with a non-Muslim government but signs begin to emerge that the latter might suddenly trick the former and attack it, still Muslims are not supposed to take any action merely on the basis of suspicion. Instead, they can openly announce the ending of the treaty by stressing that they have, till then, faithfully abided by its terms and have not made any efforts or moves to attack the other party.

Let me cite an incident in this regard from the time when Muawiyah (d 680 CE) was the ruler, as mentioned in the *Musnad* of Ahmad (16557) and the *Sunan* of Al-Tirmidhi (1590). At this time, Muawiyah's government had entered into a no-war pact with the Romans. When the pact was nearing its term, Muawiyah dispatched an army to the borders in order to suddenly attack the Romans the moment the term gave over, when the Romans would be ill-prepared for it. Just as the army was on the way towards the Roman frontier, a man appeared, galloping on a horse and crying out, '*Allahu Akbar* (Allah is the greatest)! Be loyal, do not betray!' This man was a companion of the Prophet, Amr Ibn Ambasa. He appeared before Muawiyah and said, 'It is strange! It is strange! What is happening? I have heard the Prophet say that a person who has entered into an agreement with another should not make any changes in it until its term is over.' Thereupon, Muawiyah instructed his forces to return.

Status of International Agreements in Islam

The fact that Islam stresses the brotherhood of all Muslims is well known. The *Qur'an* appeals to all Muslims to help fellow Muslims who are in distress and are suffering intolerable oppression. One verse in the *Qur'an* refers to this with regard to the cries of the oppressed Muslims of Mecca, appealing to other Muslims to fight their oppressors if they can. Thus, it says:

> And why should ye not fight in the cause of Allah and of those who, being weak, are ill-treated (and oppressed)—men, women, and children, whose cry is: "Our Lord! Rescue us from this town, whose people are oppressors; and raise for us from Thee one who will protect; and raise for us from Thee one who will help!" (4:75)

In this verse, the *Qur'an* clearly states that it is the duty of Muslims to help those of their fellow Muslims who are oppressed and victimized. Despite this, the *Qur'an* explicitly states that if a group of Muslims or a Muslim state has a peace treaty with a non-Muslim state whose Muslim citizens are oppressed and their religion is being put to test, still those Muslims or that Muslim state cannot come to their rescue. Instead, they should abide by their agreement. If they want to help the oppressed Muslims, they must first announce the dissolution of this agreement. Thus, the *Qur'an* states:

> Those who believed but did not emigrate, ye owe no duty of protection to them until they come not into exile, but if they call you for rescue in religion it is your duty to help them, except against a people with whom ye have a treaty of mutual alliance: and (remember) Allah seeth all that ye do. (8:72)

This is the basic principle of Islamic jihad.

Muslims have no need to adopt any apologetic or defensive stance on the issue of jihad. The doctrine of jihad is one of the clear proofs of the truth of Islam. Protection of humanity from the evil forces of oppression and persecution and pure intention in securing God's blessings are key dimensions of Islamic jihad. A true jihad has nothing whatsoever to do with strife, treachery and deceit that are such a central aspect of the Western inspired present international system that states continue to maintain relations with each other and formally enter into peace treaties and claim to abide by them but, at the same time, surreptitiously engage in proxy wars in order to destabilize one another.

Lamentably, today some elements are exhorting impressionable Muslim youth to renege on their commitments and pacts in the name of jihad. In this way, some of these youth are led to violate the commandments of the *Shari'ah* and the limits set by God, while also causing grave damage to the cause of Islam and its followers. These unintelligent people are not friends of Islam. Many of them, in fact, have been nurtured and are being used by the enemies of Islam, as for instance, Abu Hamzah Al-Misri and Omar Al-Bakri, who now live in Britain, and who, taking full advantage of the British Government's negligence, continuously enflame the emotions of susceptible Muslim youth by their hate-driven sermons.

Treaties and Agreements in Contemporary World

The moment a Muslim applies for a visa to visit or stay in

a non-Muslim country, he enters into what, in effect, is an agreement with the government of that country, promising it that he will not pose any threat to the lives and property of its people and that he will abide by its laws. He reiterates this promise numerous times while travelling to, and when entering, that country. Even if that country is vociferously anti-Muslim and anti-Islam, it is incumbent on that Muslim to abide by this agreement and respect the lives and properties of its inhabitants. This is because he has consciously entered into an agreement with that country's government and has assured it that he will respect its laws and the lives and properties of its citizens. Therefore, he has absolutely no excuse for using the name of Islam to revolt against that state or to violate the agreement that he has entered into with it.

If he violates this agreement and commits an act of aggression in that country, even with a good intention, he commits a crime in the eyes of Islam. For the Prophet has declared, "If a person assures someone else of protection from his side but then kills him, he will be made to hold the flag of treachery in his hand" (*Musnad Ahmad*: 21441). The same *hadith* is mentioned, along with a correct chain of transmitters, in the *Sahih Ibn Hibban* (5982), with the addition of the phrase "even if the slain person is a non-Muslim".

Another type of treaty or agreement is that which relates to citizenship. Muslim citizens of a modern non-Muslim state have, in effect, entered into an agreement with that state and its other citizens. This agreement is more important than other ordinary agreements in that the latter are generally valid only for a specified time period while the agreement related to one's citizenship lasts as long as a person retains citizenship of a given country.

Citizenship has always been understood as an agreement between an individual citizen and the state of a country whose citizen he or she is. The state and its citizens have clearly specified responsibilities vis-à-vis each other, as do the citizens of the country among and between themselves. They all agree to protect and not to harm the lives and properties of the citizens of the country. If someone declares that he does not regard it his duty to respect the life of his fellow citizens and that he is free to take their lives and property, the state of which he is a citizen will, naturally, at once declare him to be guilty of treason.

In today's world, citizenship has assumed the form of an agreement that is very wide in scope. Both the duties and responsibilities of the state as well as the commitments of its citizens have greatly expanded. In this regard, it is clear that it is not permissible for a Muslim citizen of a state wherein Muslims might even be badly oppressed and might have numerous complaints of mistreatment and discrimination to engage in any sort of violence against that country or its ordinary citizens as long as he remains a citizen of that country. At the most, he can retaliate against a particular oppressor if he is being oppressed. Of course, it is a different matter if he renounces citizenship of that country and shifts to another country, where the duties binding on a citizen of his former country do not apply to him.

As long as the Prophet and his companions remained in Mecca, they were citizens, to use a modern term, of the Meccan state. Despite the cruel oppression that they were subjected to, they lived in such a way that ordinary Meccans felt no threat from them at all. Although a few minor conflicts between some Muslims and some Meccan polytheists did occur at this time, these were individual disputes such as those that take place in any country between fellow citizens. However, when the Prophet left Mecca, his agreement with the Meccan polytheists effectively ended. The Meccan polytheists no longer enjoyed legal protection from the Muslims who had shifted to Medina, and vice versa.

Lamentably, we rarely, if ever, consider these limits, rules and principles regarding jihad as laid down in the *Shari'ah*, which are specified in the *Qur'an* and expressed in the authentic *Sunnah* of the Prophet. This is why we have been unable to apply them to our contemporary context. In this regard, many Muslims hold extremist views that are tantamount to a gross violation of the *Shari'ah*. It would not have been a matter of great surprise if these views were restricted only to some Muslim youths, who were reacting in this manner in the face of the oppression. But, when what are thought of as serious intellectual Muslim journals and magazines also toe this line, it is not just surprising and shocking but also grossly lamentable.

Let me clarify this issue by citing the response of some Muslim magazines in the wake of a controversy some years ago over the publishing of cartoons derogatory to the Prophet in Denmark. These magazines referred to some instances in the past, when inflamed and emotionally-driven Muslims had killed people who had mocked the Prophet. They presented these men as heroic examples that Muslims should emulate whenever the image of the Prophet is derided, as if this was precisely what is commanded by the *Shari'ah*.

He who derides the Prophet may deserve to be punished by law. It is only for the courts and the state, and not for individual Muslims, to decide the punishment and to inflict it in such cases. If a Muslim takes the law in his hands and kills a person for mocking the Prophet, he has committed a criminal offence. This is because in the Islamic *Shari'ah,* the imposition or execution of such a punishment can only be done by an established legal authority. This authority has not been given to any individual citizen. The emotionally-driven rhetoric of some Muslim magazines exhorting Muslims to murder traducers of the Prophet reflected faulty knowledge of Islam and proved to be a grave damage to the faith and its adherents. In the early years of Islam, it is important to note that this type of punishment was never executed by any individual person. It was done only by the recognized legal authorities.

A similar incident involved the murder by a Moroccan Muslim youth some years ago of a Dutch artiste who had painted verses of the *Qur'an* on the body of a nude female model. From the point of view of the *Shari'ah*, the act committed by the youth was wholly wrong. Yet, some Muslims unconditionally welcomed and praised it. It is true that the youth may have been motivated simply by the love for Islam, but still, the *Shari'ah* did not permit him to kill a citizen of a country with which his own country, Morocco, had a peace agreement. Furthermore, this Moroccan youth had come to Holland on a Dutch visa, which, in effect, meant that he had personally undertaken, or entered into an agreement, not to harm the lives and property of Dutch citizens in any way and to abide by Dutch laws. The *Shari'ah* did not give him permission to violate these two agreements. Hence, he was guilty of treason and of violating agreements—which Islam considers as grave crimes.

Wild emotionalism is often the enemy of reason. Besides the murder of the Dutch artiste being a crime according to the *Shari'ah*, did not the perpetrator of the crime and those Muslims who lauded him and his action realize how damaging and counter-productive, from the Muslim point of view, it was for Muslims to react to provocations with such violence? Through this sort of violence, we have not been able to stop enemies of Islam from engaging in sacrilegious acts. Instead, by staging violent demonstrations against them, Muslims have become victims of the bullets and batons of the police even in their own countries. They have become the laughing stock of the entire world. Every now and then, someone or the other engages in such provocative acts simply to see us get enraged and turn violent so that, thereby, we earn a bad name.

Instead of reacting in this way, wisdom demands that we should turn our opponents' stratagem upon themselves rather than helping to sharpen the swords that they wield against us. The intention of those evil-minded people is to spread hatred against Muslims throughout the world, particularly in the West. Hence, if we react to their provocation through violence, we will only be playing into their hands.

Necessary Preparations for War

If and when the need for Muslims to take to arms in the face of oppression arises, it is crucial for them to make sure that they have the military capacity as well as the faith and moral discipline required for this purpose. If these are insufficient, and if war would certainly result in the Muslims' defeat, then, generally speaking, they should desist from fighting. In other words, fighting becomes a duty only when the conditions are ripe for it. We have no example in the *Qur'an* and the Prophet's *Sunnah* of a believer fighting without a sword. It is true that at the Battle of Badr, the Muslims were greatly outnumbered by enemy forces, but they were helped by God and the Muslims scored an impressive victory. Muslims can only expect such divine help when they rejuvenate the spirit of Badr, and when they at least somewhat approach the level of faith and character of the Muslims who fought at Badr.

Of course, this does not mean that God's law of helping His servants has been repealed and that the believers should despair of His assistance. Not at all! If the believers lead a life of faith and servitude to God, make the upholding of God's religion as their aim in life, and sacrifice their all for this purpose, they have been promised by God that He can change their fortunes in such a way that strife can be ended in the world, and peace, justice and welfare can be established. The true believers should thus place their trust only in God.

Protection of Life and Property of Non-Combatants

While discussing the issue of jihad in the path of God, it is crucial to bear in mind that shedding blood in the course of jihad is not an end in itself. Nor is it the reason why jihad is a blessed act in God's eyes. The cause for jihad in God's path being considered a meritorious act is that it is a means for the exaltation of the true faith. The *mujahid* is beloved of God because of his willingness to sacrifice his own life and wealth in God's path. Islam considers shedding blood a crime, but regards oppression and strife as greater crimes. A true jihad aims at ridding the world of oppression and strife.

It is because of this that the Islamic *Shari'ah* stresses that in a state of war, only combatants or those who have trained to become combatants or are otherwise somehow involved in the war can be attacked or killed. No harm should befall any non-combatants.

Once, while on a battlefield, the Prophet came across the corpse of a woman. Driven to anger, the Prophet said,

'What sort of war was she fighting that she was killed?' Then, he sent a message to Khalid, who was leading the Muslim forces, instructing him to ensure that henceforth no woman, labourer or slave be slain in the course of the war (*Sunan Abu Daud*: 2669, *Musnad Ahmad*: 17158, 5923, *Sahih al-Bukhari*: 3015).

The Prophet repeatedly forbade the killing of women and children during war, as is mentioned in the books of *hadith*. According to one *hadith* report, the Prophet declared:

'Do not slay any old person, nor any child or woman. Do not cheat in matters of war booty. Be kind and charitable. God loves those who are charitable.'

The Prophet also forbade his followers from attacking the monks and mendicants of other faiths, even in the course of war. In a *hadith* recorded in the Musnad Ahmad (2723), whenever the Prophet used to dispatch an army to the battlefield, he would instruct it not to kill people worshipping in their religious places or those who served in such places. In the *Mu'wata* of Imam Malik, it is recorded that once, when the Caliph Abu Bakr (d 634 CE) dispatched Yazid Ibn Abu Sufiyan to Syria (at that time a largely Christian country) on a military expedition, he told him that he would meet people who would say that they had sacrificed the world in order to worship and serve God. He instructed him not to harm them. He also warned him not to attack or slay women, children, the aged and the infirm; not to cut down any fruit-bearing trees; not to despoil any human habitation or set on fire any orchard; and not to renege on treaties and agreements. In his collection of *hadith*, Imam Baihaqi (d 1066 CE) has attributed similar instructions to the Prophet, and although the chains of transmitters of the report he quotes in this regard are weak, because of the large number of narrators he listed, they are fairly reliable. This clearly suggests that targeting noncombatant civilians is not permissible at all in the course of a jihad.

Answer to a Troubling Question

In this context, it may be argued that on some occasions, the Prophet attacked an entire tribe and even imprisoned all its members. This means that all of them were made the target of attack. In the same way, in some instances, the Prophet captured the wealth of an entire tribe as booty. How can this be explained?

The fact is that at the time of the Prophet, whenever an entire tribe was attacked, it was because the tribe as a whole had waged war against him and his followers. In tribal societies, it is generally the case that the entire tribe, without any exception, goes to war against an opponent. This was also the practice in Arabia in the Prophet's times. That is why, in some cases, the Prophet ordered action to be taken against an entire tribe. If many of the battles fought at the time of the Prophet are understood in this light, several questions that many people have about them can be solved. In cases where one section of a tribe did not declare war against the Muslims while another did, the Prophet offered protection to the former from attack.

Mecca at the time of the Prophet was a small city-state. According to a report in the *Sahih Muslim* (1780), when, in 630 CE, the Prophet conquered Mecca, he issued a general announcement to its people, offering them safety if they remained in their homes and laid down their arms. He ordered his army not to kill the wounded or to pursue those who had fled. Except for a few war criminals, no Meccan was harassed. In other words, it was a declaration of peace and security for the lives and property of those Meccans who had not participated in fighting against the Muslims.

The principle was also acted upon throughout much of Muslim history. In the period immediately after the demise of the Prophet, when in battles fought by his companions against certain tribes, the lives and property of non-combatant members of those tribes were not harmed. They fought only against the armies of rulers, not against the common people. In fact, in many places, ordinary folk welcomed the Muslim armies with open arms since they were tired of the atrocities of their rulers, even though the latter were their co-religionists.

From this, it can be gauged that Islam strictly enjoins mercy and concern for humanity. It is clear from the practice of the Prophet that only combatants can be fought against in a jihad, and not unarmed, non-combatant non-Muslims, whose lives and properties Muslims must protect. Those who claim that in a jihad all potential combatants of the enemy can be killed, even if they have not actually participated in the fighting, have not understood the *hadith* reports related to the conduct of jihad in their entirety. Nor have they properly understood the conduct of the companions of the Prophet. To argue in this way is completely against the spirit of Islam and basic humanitarian principles. No convincing proof can be adduced for this argument from the Islamic sources.

Issue of War Booty or Spoils of War

Considerable misunderstand exists about the issue of the taking of booty (*mal-e ghanimah*) in the course of jihad. Some Orientalists even go to the extent of arguing that seizing booty or the spoils of war is the principal aim of jihad.

What exactly are the spoils of war? This is an issue that needs to be clearly understood. It is legitimate to capture the wealth of individuals one is waging war with. Prior to Islam, war was accompanied by widespread and indiscriminate looting of the vanquished party by the victorious army. There is no historical evidence of any government or ruler ever prohibiting this practice. The modern-day understanding that in a war situation, the property of ordinary citizens cannot, or should not, be touched is in line with Islamic teachings.

The Prophet clearly forbade indiscriminate looting in the course of jihad. Once, while travelling on a jihad, the

Muslim army was faced with an acute shortage of food. In order to satiate their hunger, some Muslim soldiers robbed a few goats and killed them. When the Prophet learnt of this, he was enraged, and in his anger, overturned the cauldrons in which the meat was being cooked, causing the food to spill out on the ground. Thereupon, the Prophet told the men that anything that had been robbed was even more strictly forbidden to them than eating carrion (*Abu Daud:* 2705, *Ibn Majah*: 3938). According to another *hadith* report, the Prophet declared that robbers and dacoits could not be considered to be among his followers (*Tirmidhi*: 1601).

It must be clearly understood that the spoils of war include only that wealth which is the property of the enemy state or of combatants engaged in fighting against Muslims and which falls into the hands of the Muslims during the course of a war. For a Muslim army to take their wealth and possessions either before the commencement of fighting or after the war has ended is not legitimate in Islam, and would be treated as looting, which is sternly forbidden or *haram*.

In the early Islamic period, it was a generally accepted

practice, according to the then prevalent international laws governing war that combatant soldiers could be taken as slaves and their property confiscated as spoils of war. Till such time as Muslims clashed with small tribes who lacked established governments and armies and all of whose members participated in the fighting, it was understood that the property of the entire tribe could be considered as spoils of war. For instance, this was the case with the Banu Mustalaq and the Jews of Medina and Khaybar, but despite this, the Prophet showed considerable leniency towards them. The entire tribe of Banu Hawazin fought against the Muslims. They had brought along to the battlefield even their women, children and animals. This is why all of these were considered to be spoils of war. In this context, I must also add that in some places, the Islamic state did not take any booty from the defeated, as in the case when Mecca fell to the Prophet and his forces. A large portion of the spoils of war gained from Hawazin was distributed to the Meccans, including to some of their chieftains who had spearheaded the campaign against the Muslims, several of whom had not even accepted Islam by then, while the Muslims were denied any share in them.

Later in Muslim history, when battles took place between regular armies of established governments, the situation changed. That is why it was considered that the lives and properties of ordinary, non-combatant subjects needed to be protected. When Muslim armies conquered countries that had established governments and armies, the properties of civilians were considered safe. Some Muslim fighters thought that just as the land that had fallen to the victorious Muslim armies after the Battle of Khaybar with the Jews of that town in 629 CE had been distributed among them, so too the lands captured in places like Iraq and Syria would also be given to them. However, the Caliph Umar, on the advice of other companions of the Prophet, decided that these lands must remain with their original tillers. He imposed the *kharaj* tax on the tillers, the proceeds of which were to be used for the general welfare.

It was in Iraq that this problem first emerged, and when it did, the Caliph Umar wrote to the head of the conquering Muslim army, Sa'ad Ibn Abi Waqqas, instructing him that the animals and other wealth that the Muslim army had captured should be divided into five parts, four of which were to be distributed among the soldiers, the fifth to be set apart for the government. He also added that the lands should be left with their original cultivators so that the proceeds of the taxes levied on them could be used to pay the salaries of government officials (*Futuh al-Buldan:* 265, *Al-Kharaj*: 15). These lands, contrary to what some Muslim soldiers had expected, were not distributed among the Muslims or taken over by the Muslim state as in Khaybar. They remained in the possession of those who had been cultivating them before the conquest.

There were some basic differences in the case of the spoils of war in Khaybar and in Iraq. Firstly, Khaybar was part of the Arabian peninsula, which had to be cleared of any non-Muslim presence with an independent political status. According to the *Shari'ah*, no non-Muslim community could remain in the Arabian Peninsula. That is why it was not possible for the lands of Khaybar to remain with the Jews of that town. On the other hand, Iraq was not part of the Arabian Peninsula, and it did not have the same sort of status according to the *Shari'ah*.

Secondly, Khaybar was a tribal state. In such a state, no clear distinction is made between the property of the state and that of individuals. If such a state goes to war, no distinction exists between the state and its inhabitants. I have already stated before that by keeping this point in mind, many seemingly problematic issues relating to most of the battles fought at the time of the Prophet can be solved.

In the Battle of Khaybar, all the people of Khaybar participated in the war against the Muslims. They could all be considered to have been enemies and conspirators. That is why it was legitimate and possible to seize all their properties. On the other hand, on the eve of the Muslim conquest, Iraq was a part of the vast Persian Sassanian Empire. It was ruled by a mighty, firmly-established and highly sophisticated state. Most Iraqis were tired of the cruel oppression of their Sassanian rulers. Their status was not that of combatants. In fact, many of them actually welcomed the Muslim army as liberators.

Thirdly, the lands in Khaybar had been given to the Jews only on a temporary basis, on the understanding that the Islamic state, which owned them, could take them back whenever it so wished (*Sahih al-Bukhari:* 2338, *Sahih Muslim*: 1551). This was not the case in Iraq, where the ownership of the land by the original cultivators was recognized by the new Muslim government. While some *ulema* believed that the lands in Iraq were not owned by anyone, the Muslim government as well as ordinary Muslims confirmed that they were still owned by those who had been cultivating them before the Muslim conquest. This was also the considered opinion of the jurisprudents of the Hanafi School.

In his *Tarikh-e Baghdad*, the 11th Century historian al-Khatib al-Baghdadi cites the opinion of numerous *ulema* of the first Islamic century, from which it is apparent that, from the very beginning, there were two opinions on the matter. Some *ulema* argued that the conquered lands of Iraq (and Syria etc.) should be treated as the property of the Islamic state and that their cultivators could only be considered as sharecroppers. On the other hand, another section of *ulema* believed that the original cultivators of those lands should continue to be considered their owners. In the opinion of the noted commentator on Muslim economic history, Qasim Ibn Sallam, these two opinions have always existed among the *ulema*. It is a fact, however, that Muslim governments protected the right of ownership of the lands of their original cultivators and allowed their heirs to inherit these from them. According to some scholars, Abdullah Ibn Masud, the great scholar and companion of the Prophet, and Hasan and Husain, grandsons of the Prophet, purchased lands in Iraq. This means that the cultivators of the conquered lands were recognized as owners who could sell their lands if they wished. (*Al-Amwal* of Ibn Sallam: 1/222)

Numerous modern Western scholars who have studied both early Islamic as well as Persian sources have also concluded that the Muslims allowed these lands to remain with their original cultivators as their property. In Iran, according to an entry in the *Encyclopedia Britannica*, 'Apart from the Persian elite and the Zoroastrian priests, whose property was confiscated, most of the local people were allowed to keep their possessions and their religion.' The Zoroastrian priests in Iran were part of the governing class, and they owned vast estates. This is why, in the wake of the Muslim conquest, their lands were confiscated and distributed among the poor.

The same thing happened in Syria as well. When Syria was conquered by the Muslims, the Caliph Umar sent instructions to Abu Ubaidah to let the lands remain in the possession of their original cultivators and to levy the *jizyah* tax on them. This principle was followed in subsequent Muslim conquests elsewhere, where cultivators were confirmed in the ownership of their lands, in exchange for which they had to pay the *kharaj* tax. According to the ninth century historian al-Baladhiri, when, in 641 CE, Egypt was conquered by a Muslim army, its people approached the general of the army, Amr Ibn al-'As, requesting him to let them retain ownership of their lands in return for paying the *kharaj* tax, as was the policy in Syria. This request was granted by the then Caliph. In these conquered territories, besides agricultural land, the other personal properties, both movable and immovable, of the general non-Muslim populace, including their homes, were unanimously considered to remain vested in their possession.

The crux of my argument, therefore, is that, in a jihad the spoils of war are restricted only to the property of the enemy state and its combatant soldiers.

Abolition of Oppressive Feudalism

In order to better understand the early Muslim conquests of territories that had for long been part of the Persian Sassanian and Roman Byzantine Empires, it is crucial to note that these empires were very oppressive powers and had instituted a greatly exploitative system of landlordism. Land ownership was mainly in the hands of the state, or its officers, who permitted their subjects to cultivate the lands only on the harshest conditions.

A modern historian Deno John Geanokoplos writes in his remarkable work *Byzantine: Church, Society* and *Civilization, Seen Through Contemporary Eyes* that land ownership in the Byzantine Empire was mainly in the hands of the state or its officers, who permitted the subjects to cultivate it only on the harshest conditions. In return, the state extracted revenue from the subjects in the form of fixed taxes.

It was also common for the Emperor to reward faithful officers with large estates, giving them a free hand to exploit their labourers as they wished. This was a major cause of resentment among the poor. Much land was also owned by farmer-soldiers, leaving a very limited amount of land in the form of free peasant holdings. The free peasant farmers had to bear stringent taxes, in addition to providing the military with recruits. The same oppressive feudal system existed in the Sassanid Iran. This was a major cause for resentment among the impoverished peasantry.

It is to the credit of the Muslims that when they conquered these territories, they overthrew this system and restored the lands to their cultivators. This was, in fact, one of the main reasons why, in many places, the Muslims were welcomed by the oppressed peasantry, making it even more difficult for the armies of the Roman and Persian empires to halt their advance. This was a major factor of the success of the Muslim conquests.

In our times, when the state has become a very strong and well-established institution, and where there exists a clear-cut distinction between state-owned property and that of private individuals, it can be said that in the event of a jihad, it is the right of an Islamic government to take over the property of a vanquished enemy state while, at the same time, it must protect the ownership rights of those of the latter's subjects who have not actively participated in the war.

According to the *Qur'an*, four-fifths of the wealth seized as spoils of war should be distributed among the soldiers, and the rest set aside for the government and the general welfare. Thus, it says:

> And know that out of all the booty that ye may acquire (in war),

> a fifth share is assigned to Allah and to the Messenger and to near relatives, orphans, the needy, and the wayfarer. (8:41)

Yet, as is evident from the practice of the Prophet, because he was the head of the Islamic state, God had granted him permission to act differently on account of certain considerations. This is an issue concerning jurisprudence (*fiqh*). When Mecca was conquered, the Prophet did not take any spoils of war.

After the battle of Hawazin, the Prophet did not distribute the spoils of war for a certain period. In fact, he even expressed his desire to return this wealth to the people of Hawazin if they came to him. Had they appeared before the spoils of war had been distributed, they would have got back their wealth and secured the release of their captured men. This indicates that the Prophet was entitled to exercise his discretion in the matter of the spoils of war.

Later, when the people of Hawazin came to the Prophet, he allowed them to choose between taking their wealth or their captured people back (*Sahih al-Bukhari*: 4319). This shows that the Prophet, as a ruler of the state, was allowed to make his own decisions about the spoils of war. If it were absolutely essential to distribute them as booty among the

Muslim army, he would not have been able to give the people of Hawazin this choice. The Prophet gave nothing at all from the spoils of war to the majority of those Muslims who had participated in the battle of Hawazin. Instead, he distributed it mainly to soften the hearts of others who had not participated in the war, including some who actually wanted that the Muslims be vanquished. A large number of these people were not even Muslims at that time (*Tabqat Ibn Sa'ad*: 150/2).

Some biographers of the Prophet labour under the mistaken impression that distributing the spoils of war among the *mujahids* is an inflexible law. They argue that the portion of the spoils of war from the Battle of Hawazin that the Prophet gave to some people to soften their hearts was from the fifth portion that had been set apart for the state. But this claim is not reliable. According to Hafiz Ibn Qayyim (d 1328 CE), in the wake of the Battle of Hunayn in 630 CE, the spoils of war were not distributed among the *mujahids*. Thus, the arguments given by some about the division of the spoils of the Battle of Hawazin are not correct. They are not in accordance with authentic records of the event. Several sources relate that the spoils of war from the Battle of Hawazin were entirely distributed to the Quraish of Mecca and those whose hearts had to be softened, and that nothing at all was given to the Ansar, the Muslims of Medina. Some sources claim that nothing was given to the Muhajirs, the Muslims of Mecca, and this is the correct opinion.

Likewise, according to Abdullah Bin Zaid, the spoils of war from the Battle of Hunayn were entirely distributed among those whose hearts had to be softened, and nothing was given to the Ansar (*Sahih al-Bukhari:* 4330). Those whose hearts had to be softened who received a share of the spoils of war were numerous, and it is evident that they together received much more than the fifth share that was set apart for the state to disburse.

The *Qur'an* clearly establishes:

> They ask thee concerning (things taken as) spoils of war. Say: "(Such) spoils are at the disposal of Allah and the Messenger: so fear Allah, and keep straight the relations between yourselves: Obey Allah and His Messenger, if ye do believe". (8:1)

This means that the *Qur'an* allows for the possibility for the spoils of war not to be distributed among the *mujahids*. Scholars of the *Qur'an* know that the phrase 'Allah and the

Messenger' appears on some occasions in the *Qur'an* to refer to the government or the established political authority because in the Prophet's time, all political power was in the hands of the Prophet, as God had willed.

Besides the examples that I have mentioned, in other cases too the Prophet distributed the spoils of war in accordance with his own judgment or *ijtihad*, in line with the power bestowed on him by God. This is why, in the wake of the Battle of Khaybar, he provided some people who had come from Yemen and Ethiopia the same share in the spoils of war as the *mujahids* although they had not participated in the war (*Sahih al-Bukhar*i: 3136).

The conduct of the Prophet and the instructions in the above-quoted Qur'anic verse need to be carefully understood. At the time of the Prophet, armies consisted of volunteers. They would arrange for their own weapons and food, and would bear their own expenses while marching on a campaign. Since today regular armies are well-paid by their governments and enjoy many other privileges, the matter of the spoils of war needs to be re-examined, and in this regard modern customs and practices must also be considered.

Prisoners of War

The Prophet recommended that prisoners of war be treated with kindness and concern. The *Qur'an* mentions about people who deserve to enter heaven thus:

> And they feed, for the love of Allah, the indigent, the orphan and the captive—(Saying) "We feed you for the sake of Allah alone: no reward do we desire from you, nor thanks". (76:8–9)

In the wake of the Battle of Badr, because of the Prophet's exhortations his companions provided their prisoners of war even better food than they had themselves. One of these prisoners was fed bread and curry, while the people in whose house he was kept survived merely on dates. Taken aback by this kind treatment, he offered to eat dates and let the members of that family eat the bread and curry instead. The man of the house turned down this suggestion, saying that the Prophet had taught the Muslims to treat their prisoners of war well (*Sirat Ibn Hisham*: 1/675).

From the *Qur'an,* it is evident that Muslims were not given permission to take captives in war until they were fully victorious over their enemies. Although the Meccan polytheists had suffered a defeat at the Battle of Badr, their power had not been shattered. They had fled from the battle, but yet they had not been fully vanquished. They could still carry on with their plots and attacks against the Muslims. When the Meccans started fleeing the battlefield, the Muslim soldiers began capturing them in the hope of earning a handsome ransom. In this period, there was no system for detaining captured enemy soldiers until war had ceased. It is in this context that one should view the Qur'anic commandment not to take prisoners of war until and unless the enemy had been fully and decisively defeated. The *Qur'an* warned the Muslims not to do so simply in order to earn ransom, because this would not, in any way, completely destroy the power of the enemy. Instead, it exhorted them to continue fighting till the strength of the enemy had been shattered. Thus, the *Qur'an* says:

> It is not fitting for an apostle that he should have prisoners of war until he hath thoroughly subdued the land. Ye look for the temporal goods of this world; but Allah looketh to the Hereafter; and Allah is Exalted in might Wise. (8:67)

Before this verse had been revealed, the *Qur'an* had instructed the Muslims to seek to fully vanquish the deniers of the truth in the battlefield if they were forced by them to go to war, and only after that could they take prisoners of war. As for these prisoners, the Muslims were told to release them as a gesture of generosity or to exchange them for Muslims who had been taken prisoner by the enemy or else to set them free in lieu of some payment. As the *Qur'an* put it:

> Therefore, when ye meet the Unbelievers (in fight), smite at their necks; at length, when ye have thoroughly subdued them, bind a bond firmly (on them): therefore (is the time for) either generosity or ransom: until the war lays down its burdens. (47:4)

From these two Qur'anic verses, it is clear that the rationale of the prohibition on taking prisoners of war until the enemy is fully vanquished is to make Muslims seek the complete subjugation of their enemies. But if, as in modern times, it is possible for prisoners of war to be detained till the enemy is fully defeated and the war is over, it may be permissible to do so.

Issue of Slavery

The above-mentioned Qur'anic verses instruct Muslims to release their captives of war out of benevolence or for a ransom. This is the basic Islamic rule. The issue now arises of why, in the some of the wars that he fought, the Prophet enslaved the men and women of the defeated tribes. This practice was continued, although in a very limited way, in the period of the Caliphs after his demise. Why was this? How was this justifiable?

It is necessary to discuss this issue in detail, but in this book I can do so only briefly. While seeking to understand the matter, it must be borne in mind that the *Qur'an* referred to slavery as an existing social institution in those times, but there is no mention of slavery in the rules of war that it elaborates on at length. In fact, it provides only three options to with regard to prisoners of war—that they are released with kindness, or for a ransom, or in exchange for prisoners of war kept in the custody of their enemy, which is a form of ransom. Thus, the *Qur'an* lays down, in a verse quoted above:

> Therefore, when ye meet the Unbelievers (in fight), smite at their necks; at length, when ye have thoroughly subdued them, bind a bond firmly (on them): therefore (is the time for) either generosity or ransom: until the war lays down its burdens. (47:4)

This verse does not allow the option for keeping prisoners of war as slaves. In the same way, there is no mention in the corpus of *hadith*, at least as far as I know, of enslaving people in the course of a war as an established law. It is true that the Prophet did enslave some people after he had defeated them in battle. But, he released most of them soon after in kindness, and some in return for ransom or in exchange for Muslim prisoners of war who had been taken by their enemies. This was his basic practice. Thus, for instance, in the wake of the Battle of Badr, when the Muslims had taken numerous prisoners of war, the Prophet released some of them in kindness, but the majority for a ransom.

Prior to the Treaty of Hudaibiyah, a group of some 80 Meccans attacked the Muslims, and all of them were taken as prisoners. The Prophet released them without any a ransom (*Sahih Muslim*: 1808). When the Prophet finally conquered Mecca, he set free everyone. Thus, enslaving captives was only a very rare practice.

The Muslim army captured some 6,000 people of Hawazin in the wake of a fierce war. The people of Hawazin were inveterate foes of the Muslims. The Prophet waited for a fortnight for the leaders of the Hawazin to yield and seek their release. Had he released them at once, they would surely have gone back to join the ranks of the enemy. This is why the Prophet did not distribute the spoils of war and the captives that had been taken in the fighting. When, after waiting for many days, the leaders of Hawazin did not appear, he distributed the captives among the Muslims, because there was no other means to maintain them.

Two weeks or so after that, some people from Hawazin appeared before the Prophet and pleaded with him to return to them their people and their wealth. The Prophet allowed them to choose between taking back their captured men and their confiscated wealth. They requested him to give them the men. These men had already been distributed as slaves among the Muslims, but the Prophet ordered their release (*Sahih al-Bukhari*: 2608, 4319).

In addition to this example, the corpus of *hadith* is replete with instances of prisoners of war being released. Thus, enslaving prisoners was a rare exception, rather than the rule. In the period of the 'Righteous Caliphs', too, this remained the case, with prisoners of war being generally released in return for them paying the *jizyah* tax and the *kharaj* levy on their lands.

Prior to the Qur'anic revelation, no code of law in the entire world forbade slavery or condemned the enslavement of prisoners of war. In seeking to understand the cases wherein the Prophet, or after him the early Muslims, did turn prisoners into slaves, it must be remembered that if these people had been immediately released while war continued and the enemy had not accepted to obey the Prophet, they would have gone back to join the enemy's ranks. Civilization had not developed at that time to such an extent as to maintain jails for such prisoners and for the state to bear the cost of feeding and maintaining them. That is why, in these cases, enslaving prisoners was a compulsion, and not an established law regulating the conduct of war in Islam.

It must also be borne in mind that the abolition of the institution of slavery throughout the world was a gradual process, a result of the development of man's social consciousness and his social and economic development. At the time of the Prophet, and not just in Arabia alone but in large parts of the rest of the world as well, slavery was an unfortunate, but yet existing social reality. It is to the credit of the Islamic *Shari'ah* that it, in effect, removed slavery from its basic law, and stressed that prisoners of war should be released in kindness or for a ransom or in exchange for

Muslims who had been taken captive by the enemy.

It is true that in a very few cases at the time of the Prophet, some prisoners of war were indeed made into slaves. But this, as I mentioned earlier, was an exception, born out of compulsion, and a fully understandable one, given the fact that the Prophet's enemies too refused to give up the practice of enslaving their prisoners of war. Had Islam unilaterally refused to do so in practice, it would have further emboldened the enemy, who would no longer fear being enslaved by Muslims while they continued to keep Muslim captives as slaves. To reiterate, the few cases of non-Muslim captives being enslaved by the Prophet were a compulsion, given the then prevailing situation. It was certainly not what could be called the basic or essential Islamic law or rule.

From this discussion, it emerges that slavery, or making prisoners slaves is not a part of the Islamic law of war. Islam has not given this practice any sort of continued or permanent legitimacy. At the time of the Prophet and the early Muslims, there was simply no other way to keep and maintain prisoners of war, and that is why some of them were made slaves. This was something done under compulsion and as an exception. Today, when this compulsion no longer exists because human civilization has considerably advanced, there can be no justification for slavery.

In today's context, the Islamic ruling would be to keep captives of war in prisons as long as is considered necessary according to the requirements of war, and then to release them in kindness or for a ransom or in exchange for Muslims taken captive by the enemy.

In this regard, one must also consider the legal rights that Islam provided to slaves and the great stress that it laid on dealing kindly with them. The *Qur'an* describes the freeing of slaves as an act of great merit and piety, and repeatedly appeals to Muslims to do so. On numerous occasions, the *Qur'an* calls for the manumission of slaves. It stresses that if slaves are able and willing to pay for their freedom, they should be released. The *Qur'an* also orders Muslims and the Muslim political authorities to financially help slaves who wish to be released from their masters in return for a certain sum of money.

A tradition recorded in the *Sahih of al-Bukhari* relates that once, during the Caliphate of Umar, a slave of Anas offered to pay him for his release, but he refused. The slave then approached Umar and sought his help. In turn, Umar instructed Anas to release him. Many *ulema* believe that the Qur'anic order to release slaves in this way was not compulsory to follow, only merely something laudable, but the Caliph Umar and many other Islamic scholars interpreted it as compulsory and binding.

According to Islamic teachings, slaves must be looked after kindly and properly. Islam even insists that slaves and their masters should enjoy almost same standard of living or at least that there should not be a major difference between them in this regard. They should eat the same sort of food and wear the same sort of clothes. Once Abudhar, a companion of the Prophet, scolded his slave. On learning about this, the Prophet was enraged, and said, "Abudhar! The remnants of the days of ignorance (*jahiliyah*) are still within you. These slaves are your brothers. God has given them to you, so behave kindly with them. You must give them what you eat. You must give them the same sort of clothes that you wear. Give them work that is easy to do, or else assist them in their work" (*Sahih al-Bukhari*: 30).

The Prophet asked people to give good education and moral training to their slaves and even to free their women slaves and marry them (*Sahih al-Bukhari*: 97). Numerous other *hadith* reports relate such instructions.

As a result of these teachings, in many cases, slaves in Muslim societies were treated well. Some of them even became teachers, guides, religious leaders, ministers, military commanders, governors of provinces, and even monarchs. There have been several 'slave dynasties' among Muslims, which ruled over vast territories.

Other Humanitarian Laws Governing War

From our discussion so far, it is clear that Islam has sought to regulate war through various humanitarian and moral codes and rules. Because war involves violence and bloodshed, in its essence it is something impermissible, and, as a principle, forbidden (*haram*). Islam stresses respect for humankind and the protection of human life. It regards war as only an exception to this general rule, if the need so arises. The *Qur'an* explains this by saying that even more dangerous than warfare is to forbid, through force and coercion, people from following the religion of truth and to torment and brutally oppress such people. This is the Qur'anic rationale for war. While allowing for war or enjoining it, as an exception and under unavoidable circumstances, Islam sought to control it through certain laws and regulations. Thus, according to a *hadith* report, the Prophet announced that God has ordered good behaviour at all times, even while taking the life of a human or an animal (*Sahih Muslim*: 1900).

Islam forbids the mutilation and dishonouring of the bodies of enemy soldiers slain in fighting (*Sahih al-Bukhari*: 2474). Whenever the Prophet dispatched his followers on a military expedition, he would ask them to fear God, and not to break their oaths or cheat or mutilate bodies while fighting (*Sahih Muslim*: 1731). If someone engages in such acts he is not fit to be called a *mujahid*. Nor can he receive the merit of participating in jihad. Instead, he would be destined for hell. The aim of jihad in Islam is not to conquer lands or for Muslims to establish their political hegemony. Rather, the only rationale for jihad is to remove the hurdles placed in the path of inviting people to the path of God, to end persecution, and to enable the upholders of Truth to guide and serve humanity. This is why when the Caliph Abu Bakr dispatched the first Muslim army after the demise of the Prophet, headed by Usama Ibn Zaid, he instructed

Zaid not to deceive anyone, not to rob the spoils of war, not to renege on any agreements, not to dismember the corpses of enemy soldiers, not to kill children, women, the aged, monks and people serving in places of worship, not to cut down trees and orchards, and not to unnecessarily kill the animals belonging to others (*Tarikh Al-Tabari*: 6/246).

In the course of war Islam forbids indiscriminate slaughter, the killing of non-combatants, the setting on fire to properties and engaging in general destruction. In this regard, the Prophet said:

"Wars are of two types. He, who fights for the sake of God's acceptance and pleasure, obeys the commander, sacrifices his dear possessions in God's path, behaves well with his companions, and stays away from strife and destruction, his sleeping and awakening are in God's path and a source of blessing. But he who sets out to fight simply for show, disobeys the commander, and spreads destruction and chaos, not only will not get any merit, but, on the contrary, will return having committed a sin" (*Sunan an-Nasai*: 3137, *Musnad Ahmad*: 21537).

This indicates that destroying buildings, fields and orchards and public utilities in the course of war is not permitted in Islam, unless this is indispensable to encircle the enemy or to break through a siege.

The tribe of Banu Nadir had entered into a pact with the Muslims, but later reneged on the agreement and even tried to kill the Prophet. This led to the Battle of Banu Nadir, in the course of which the Muslims set on fire some orchards that surrounded the fort of the enemy (*Sahih al-Bukhari:* 4031, *Sahih Muslim*: 1746). This was done because it was a necessary military tactic. It was an exception under the circumstances, not a general rule. Some people have misunderstood this and believe that this signified a general permission to engage in this sort of action. Their view is undoubtedly wrong, and is not sanctioned under Islam's doctrine of war.

Evidence of this view being erroneous is clearly suggested by the fact that whenever the Caliph Abu Bakr dispatched a Muslim army on a military expedition, he would warn its soldiers not to cut or burn down fruit-bearing trees and orchards or to lay waste human habitations. When he issued these instructions to the Muslim armies, none of the other companions of the Prophet raised any objection. This is proof that the Prophet's companions believed that it was not permissible to engage in indiscriminate destruction of the wealth and property of the enemy. In the *Mu'wata* (858) and the *Sunan Baihaqi* (90/9), there are similar narrations attributed to the Prophet himself. Although their chains of narrators are weak, because their number is considerable, the great scholar of *hadith* Imam Baihaqi regarded them as reliable.

Most Islamic scholars also agreed with the Caliph Abu Bakr's instructions not to cut or burn down trees and orchards belonging to the enemy in the course of a war, unless in an extreme necessity or as a military tactic to overcome the enemy. Accordingly, in his *Sunan*, Imam Tirmidhi (d 892 CE) approvingly quoted the scholar Al-Auzai as having said, 'To cut down trees and set fire on orchards etc., is prohibited. The Caliph Abu Bakr has forbidden this, and Muslims have acted on this instruction.'

This quotation is very important, for it indicates that although the early Muslims fought several battles, they did not, with certain exceptions and that too out of military compulsion, burn down orchards or cut down trees belonging to the people whom they fought. The noted Hanafi jurisprudent Ibn al-Humam was of the view that such acts can be resorted to only when they are indispensable for taking on the enemy. He argued that if this is not the case they are forbidden on the grounds that it would cause chaos and oppression (*Fath al-Qadeer*: 5/197). This argument is also recorded in important Hanafi *fiqh* texts as *Shami* and others, and in the well-known Hanbali text *Kashhaf al-Qina'a* and its commentary, which add that these acts can also be resorted to if the enemy engages in the same so that the enemy might desist from such acts in the future. Some writers claim that Imam Ahmad Ibn Hanbal (d 855 CE) permitted the destruction of enemy property in the course of war, but this is a misunderstanding. Rather, he permitted this only if there was a compelling need for it, as has been related by Imam Tirmidhi.

The *Kashhaf al-Qina'a* lays down that burning down fields and orchards or destroying the property of ordinary people is permitted only if this is a military necessity, but is otherwise forbidden. The noted scholar Imam Ibn Jarir Tabari explains that such acts must not aim at spreading destruction and desolation, and that if they are so intended they are forbidden. All this indicates that the views of those Islamic scholars who justify such acts must be seen as being strictly limited to situations of extreme military necessity, and not as a general permission to engage in such acts, for that would be totally against the spirit of the *Shari'ah*.

Another important rule with regard to the conduct of war in Islam is that the life of emissaries must be protected and they must also be given due respect. This is what the Prophet taught. Whenever emissaries from other states or tribes came to him, he would present them with gifts. Once, two emissaries appeared before the Prophet, sent by Musailimah the Liar, a false claimant to divinity, who was an enemy of the Islamic state. They were both guilty of apostasy, mutiny and treason, and thus deserved to be killed. But the Prophet said, 'It is not permissible to kill emissaries', adding that otherwise he would have had them killed (*Musnad Ahmad:* 3752, *Sunan Abu Daud*: 2763).

Towards the end of his life, when the Prophet was struck by what proved to be a fatal illness, he issued a set of instructions that were meant to be followed by the future leaders of the Muslims. One of these was, 'Present emissaries with gifts, just as I used to' (*Sahih Bukhari*: 4431).

Six

Non-violent Forms of Jihad

THE DOCTRINE of jihad can be said to be one of the proofs of the truth of Islam. The aim of jihad is to establish peace, welfare and justice in society, and *mujahids*, those who partake in jihad, are people who are inspired by firm faith in God and follow His commandments. They are motivated not by lust for the world, but rather for reward in the Hereafter. Their fear of Allah restrains them from all forms of injustice and oppression. Preparing such a group of committed people is in itself a form of jihad as is the struggle that they participate in, for which they are willing to sacrifice their lives. Their sacrifice is more valuable than all the good and pious deeds that the whole world contains.

This is why the Prophet referred to jihad as the highest form of goodness. This is also why the *Qur'an* says:

> Those who believed and those who suffered exile and fought (and strove and struggled) in the path of God—they have the hope of the Mercy of God: And God is Oft-forgiving, Most Merciful. (2:218)

According to a tradition recorded in the *Sahih al-Bukhari* (2792), the worth of spending one day and one evening in the path of jihad is more than that of the entire world and all that it contains and all the other things bestowed by God. According to another *hadith* report, it is better that a person sets out on jihad than if he were to spend 70 years in his house praying (*Sunan Tirmidhi*: 1650). The *Qur'an* explains that war sometimes becomes inevitable for the sake of the establishment of truth and justice, when without war the bloody crimes committed by oppressors cannot be halted and their attempts to block the invitation to God's path cannot be rebuffed. Under such conditions, war becomes a duty incumbent upon those who walk in God's path and seek paradise. As the *Qur'an* puts it:

> Unless ye do this (jihad), there would be tumult and oppression on earth, and great mischief. (8:73)

In God's eyes, true Muslims are those who are immersed

in His service, for whom this is the very reason for existence, and for which cause they engage in struggle. God has promised them paradise in exchange for this service. If they abdicate this struggle, God will consider them to be oath-breakers (9:111–112). This is to say that in God's eyes true believers are those who have firm faith in God and His Prophet and do not doubt their promises and who struggle in God's path with their wealth and their lives. This is why the Prophet stressed that the desire for jihad is an essential condition for true faith (49:15).

Forms of Jihad other than War

The actual aim of jihad in the path of God is to help the cause of the true religion, to help those who follow the truth, and to struggle against the forces of persecution and oppression through arms if need be. However, if there is no oppression of this sort, striving in the path of God will still continue, but by using other means. This would be considered jihad in the path of God in that particular context. Those who participate in this non-violent jihad for the sake of winning God's acceptance and do not hesitate to make sacrifices for this will get the same blessings from

God as those who, in a different context, participate in physical struggle against oppression.

When the Prophet emigrated from Mecca to Medina and the possibility of war with the enemies of the Muslims arose, sacrificing one's life and property for the sake of God by participating in physical jihad assumed the highest form of jihad. Those Muslims who stayed away from this sort of jihad were treated as hypocrites or as weak in faith. Yet, before this, when the Muslims were in Mecca and were not then required to take part in physical fighting, a time when they were subjected to oppression and social boycott and were denied religious freedom, their jihad for that period was for them to remain steadfast in the face of the difficult conditions that they faced, to refuse to submit to the forces of infidelity and oppression, and to firmly abide by their faith. At that time, their basic mission was to establish the worship and service of God and lead a pure life—a life of faith and total submission to God.

Forms of Jihad when Armed Jihad is not Needed

The *Qur'an* indicates that a major mission of the Muslims in Medina, after they had migrated from Mecca, was to physically fight with their oppressive enemies, to engage in jihad as physical war. In exactly the same way, the *Qur'an* declares that in the period prior to this, when the Muslims were still in Mecca, their major mission was to remain steadfast in their commitment to the truth, to bravely face the many hurdles in that path, and to refuse to bow down before the forces of infidelity and oppression. In this difficult mission, the *Qur'an* made the establishment of worship (*salat*) and service of God as the basis of a life of faith, as their source of inspiration, and as the means for victory in the face of terrible odds. The *Qur'an* indicates that this peaceful jihad was the actual mission of the Muslims in that context. Thus, while the Prophet was in Mecca, before he and his companions migrated to Medina, the following Qur'anic verse, using the term 'jihad', was revealed:

> Therefore listen not to the Unbelievers, but strive (do jihad) against them with the utmost strenuousness, with the [*Qur'an*]. (25:52)

The following verse was also revealed in the Meccan period:

> Do men think that they will be left alone on saying "We believe" and that they will not be tested? We did test those before them, and Allah will certainly know those who are true

> from those who are false [...] And if any strive [jihad], they do so for their own souls: for Allah is free of all needs from all creation. (29:2–6)

In this verse, the *Qur'an* points out that mere verbal confession of faith is not enough. It says that God will test people and only then can they be admitted to heaven. It refers to the case of earlier communities, who were similarly tried by God by making them face difficult situations in order to gauge their faith and commitment. Referring to the Muslims in Mecca at that time, it said that they too would be similarly tested so that God may know who was truly committed to His religion and who was not. It indicates that those who face and suffer immense difficulties but yet remain steadfast and strong in their faith are engaged in a form of jihad. In his commentary on this verse, the noted scholar Hafiz Ibn Kathir (d 1373 CE) refers to Imam Hasan al-Basri as having said, "Undoubtedly, a person who has never wielded a sword also sometimes engages in jihad."

In the same chapter, where the above-mentioned verse is mentioned, the *Qur'an* further adds:

> And those who strive (do jihad) in Our (Cause)—We will

> certainly guide them to Our Paths: for verily Allah is with those who do right. (29:69)

In these verses, the *Qur'an* uses the term 'jihad' to refer to the peaceful struggle of Muslims in the face of oppression and persecution.

From these Qur'anic verses, it is evident that in circumstances when physical jihad is not needed or not possible for any group of Muslims, their jihad will be to remain faithful to God and His religion, to be steadfast in their commitment to establishing worship and doing good deeds, and to make the promotion of their life of faith their mission. This is their duty and this is their jihad. This clearly suggests that there are indeed forms of jihad other than fighting in a war.

God's Promise to Help the *Mujahids*

The *Qur'an* promises the *mujahids* that God will assist them. What is the unchangeable practice (*sunnat*) and law of God in this regard? Who are promised such assistance and when? When do Muslims get disqualified from receiving such assistance? When, in accordance with His practice, does God cause them to be abased and become weak and fall prey at the hands of oppressors? And, in today's context, in which way is this unchangeable practice of God being expressed?

In the *Qur'an,* God repeatedly stresses that He will certainly arrange for heavenly assistance to those who believe in His prophets, lead the life that true believers should, and work for spreading worship and service of God and goodness and welfare in the world even if they face opposition from His enemies. Helping those who abide by the Truth is a fixed and established practice of God. Even if such people have few material resources to combat their oppressors, God will provide them the means from the Unseen to be victorious.

In the Battle of Uhud in 625 CE, the Muslims were defeated, but yet the *Qur'an* told them not to grieve, and assured them that they would be victorious if they were truly faithful (3:139). In the *Surah Al-Haj* of the *Qur'an*, God granted permission to the Muslims to engage in war and encouraged them to do so, and also referred to this unchangeable Divine law:

> Allah will certainly aid those who aid His (cause); for verily Allah is Full of Strength, Exalted in Might, (Able to enforce His Will). (22:40)

In this regard, it must be kept in mind that the promise of help and victory that the *Qur'an* makes in these verses is with regard to a group of people of true faith, correct belief and upright character, whose hearts are filled with the light of God and who lead a life according to His Will. The *Qur'an* specifies that the people who receive God's assistance are those who faithfully worship, serve, and remember Him, who do good deeds, who promote good in the world, and who spread the teachings of the prophets. They are pious people who help the poor. They are such people that if God assists them to gain power, they will remain steadfast in their mission and will not stray from it.

It must also be noted that wherever in the *Qur'an* God has promised to provide His assistance, it is for those who are called *al-muminin*, which is an Islamic term to denote the people of true faith and upright conduct, and not simply those who claim to be 'Muslims'. Scholars of the *Qur'an* know the crucial distinction between these two terms. A noted Islamic scholar, the late Maulana Manzur Nomani, elaborates on this by stressing that according to the *Qur'an*, the *muminin* are God's special servants who are firm in faith and in following His commandments in their lives. To consider the present-day Muslim community as synonymous with the *muminin* and to believe that they would receive the same sort of Divine help that the *Qur'an* promises the *muminin* reveals a lack of proper understanding of the Qur'anic idiom.

On the other hand, if a community accepts God and His Prophet and agrees to follow them but then disobeys them and breaks its covenant with God, then, according to the unchangeable practice of God, it will become a victim of His wrath. God will cause such a people to be debased, helpless, and oppressed in this world. They will be punished by Him through various torments, including harsh suppression and slaughter at the hands of oppressors.

The question now arises as to how this practice of God is being expressed in our world today. Over the last two centuries, in large parts of the world, Muslims have suffered considerable ignominy and oppression. Those who have a good understanding of the *Qur'an* know that this is a manifestation of the unchangeable practice of God. This is the answer to the question that is often asked as to why, when the *Qur'an* is replete with promises of God's help, such help is not evident today.

In the *Qur'an*, God describes this practice of His in great detail in the context of the history of the Children of Israel. The Children of Israel were descendants of various prophets. In their time, they were the custodians of God's scripture and heavenly commandments. For centuries, they enjoyed the same status as the Muslim *ummah* occupies today. The *Qur'an* provides a detailed description of how, despite this status of theirs, they disobeyed God, because of which for a long time they were punished by God, including being killed by their enemies. The *Qur'an* repeatedly mentions that the disgrace and helplessness that they had to suffer was imposed on them as a punishment from God.

In this context, the *Qur'an* refers to a group from among the Children of Israel who had accepted God and His commandments but later became a victim of their own lusts so that they accepted only those commandments that did not go against their desires, ignoring the rest. After describing this, the *Qur'an* states that God's punishment for such a crime is that those who are guilty of this offence will suffer debasement and ignominy in this world as well as stern punishment in the Hereafter (2:85). This means that whenever any community accepts God's religion but later strays from its path, in the same way as this group among the Children of Israel did, they will have to face the same fate as punishment from God. The *Qur'an* explains that this punishment can also take the form of their enemies entering their lands, engaging in widespread bloodshed, and compelling them to lead a life of despair.

When the Children of Israel exceeded all bounds in their obstinacy and rebellion against God and even began engaging in polytheism, God announced that they would certainly be punished by Him and that they would have to face disgrace in this world. God declared that this was the punishment for those who behaved in this despicable manner (2: 152). This clearly indicates that it is God's unshakable and established practice and law that if those who accept His faith and His messengers begin to tamper with their religion and invent innovations that lead to associating partners with God, they will certainly face debasement in this world as well as God's wrath. This is a warning to us today. Let those many people belonging to the *ummah* of the Prophet Muhammad who openly engage in associating partners of God, and that too in the name of Islam itself, seriously ponder on this matter.

This issue concerning the communities of the various prophets and the practice of God with regard to them has a deep relation with the question of jihad. Without understanding this, one cannot properly appreciate the principles and rules of God's help to true *mujahids*. Lamentably, the collective character of Muslims today has left no possibility open to hope that their present debasement and troubles are not the result of God's wrath.

Why didn't God's Help Appear?

One can argue that today, even if a group of Muslim *mujahids* emerges who are faithful to God's religion, deeply pious and willing to sacrifice their all for His cause, still, in accordance with God's practice, they may not be able to expect such help from God as would enable them to destroy the chains of infidelity and oppression and bring back the Muslim *ummah* to a position of respect and authority. This is because the entire Muslim community, in general, is today characterized by disloyalty to God's religion. In this regard, the true faith and commitment of just a small group of *mujahids* among the entire community cannot change the Muslims' collective fate. It may be that this small group can win some battles on account of their sacrifices or resources. However, there is no way that the collective condition of the Muslims can be changed other than for them to abide by their treaty of faith with God, which they have broken.

In the recent past, when the *mujahids* in Afghanistan were forced to suffer defeat, I, like many others, wondered why God's assistance had not come to them. One reply to this is to compare their situation with that which prevailed soon after the Battle of Uhud, when, in the presence of the Prophet himself, some people, driven by worldly desires, disobeyed him, which caused God to take back His assistance. This caused the battle, which had almost been won by the Muslims, to turn into a defeat, in which 70 companions of the Prophet were martyred and the Prophet was grievously injured. The *Qur'an* explains that this came about because some of the Muslim soldiers were driven by worldly desires. At the same time, the *Qur'an* says that if, henceforth, Muslims walk on the path of faith steadfastly, this defeat might prove to be temporary and that they may later win a conclusive victory. So, when, in the presence of the Prophet himself, some Muslims committed a blunder, driven by the lure of the world, and this caused God to withdraw his help, how can our many mistakes and errors today give us hope for any assured and immediate divine help?

From a deep study of the *Qur'an,* it emerges that God's special help that enables a community to establish its authority despite possessing limited resources and means depends on the general or collective moral conditions and faith-based character of that community. It depends on the extent to which the community has truly become the 'Party of God' (*hizbullah*), that is to say a special group of servants of God whose mission is to spread welfare in the world, whose lives are that of true *mumins*, and who, if granted power and wealth, will use them to establish worship of God, wipe out oppression, and help the poor. Such divine assistance shall not be given to a group that is goaded by worldly desires and that wants to replace an oppressive ruling community by another community that is not much different from the former in terms of character and mission. In the case of the present-day Muslims, there may be some small groups who deserve divine assistance owing to their high moral calibre and faith, but our general condition is sadly characterized by revolt and rebellion against God.

To conclude, the answer to the question as to why Muslims are suffering across the world when God has promised His true believers help from the Unseen is that such help depends on the collective moral and faith-based character of a community as a whole, and not on the faith and sincerity of a small group of *mujahids* among them.

Seven

Islamic Teachings about Relations with Non-Muslims

THE ISSUE of what Islam has to say about inter-community relations is one about which much misunderstanding exists. Anti-Muslim propagandists claim that Islam preaches hatred for non-Muslims, and that the *Qur'an* is a menace to world peace. They go so far as to argue that world peace is simply impossible as long as the *Qur'an* exists. In order to back their propaganda, they deliberately twist and misinterpret certain verses of the *Qur'an*. Many people with little knowledge have fallen prey to this poisonous propaganda, which has been aggressively spread on an enormous scale through the mass media.

At the same time, we must also admit that some Muslims themselves entertain misunderstandings and uphold extremist views about the issue of relations between Muslims and others that are based on a completely wrong interpretation of the *Qur'an* and the Prophet's *sunnah*. This calls for a detailed study so that misunderstandings, wrong interpretations and extremist views about Islamic teachings regarding relations between Muslims and others can be countered.

It is true that Islam stresses that Muslims should not be negatively influenced by others in their religious views and moral attributes, and that they should maintain their religious and moral distinctiveness. It cautions them from imitating others, especially their religious symbols and rituals which Islam does not accept. It is also true that Islam strictly forbids befriending enemies of Islam and those who conspire against Muslims. At the same time, however, Islam exhorts Muslims to relate to other non-Muslims with softness, good manners, gentleness, and love.

Respect for Humanity

Islam teaches us that all human beings, irrespective of community and race, are children of the same set of primal parents, and so are bound together by their common humanity. As the *Qur'an* states:

> O mankind! We created you from a single (pair) of a male and a female, and made you into nations and tribes, that ye may know each other (not that ye may despise each other). (49:13)

This basic Islamic teaching about the whole of humankind being children of the same parents stresses the need for consciousness of our common humanity and of us being brethren unto each other. This is why, according to a *hadith* report, the Prophet would, after finishing his prayers, supplicate with God, saying, "O Allah! Sustainer of myself and of everything! I bear witness that all human beings are brothers of each other" (*Sunan Abu Daud*: 1508).

According to the *Qur'an*, human beings are creatures worthy of respect:

> We have honoured the sons of Adam [...] and conferred on them special favours, above a great part of Our Creation. (17:70)

This clearly indicates that Islam regards human beings as deserving respect, love and concern on the basis of their humanity. A *hadith* report well illustrates this teaching. Once, the Prophet was present along with some of his disciples when a funeral procession passed by. Thereupon, the Prophet stood up. Seeing the Prophet stand out of respect for the dead man, some of his companions informed him that the man had been a Jew. But the Prophet responded, "Was he not a human being?" After the Prophet, some of his companions too followed this example of his (*Sahih al-Bukhari*: 1313).

In another *hadith* report, the Prophet exhorted his followers to relate with kindness to all creatures thus:

"God is merciful to those who are merciful. Deal with mercy towards creatures on earth and He in the heavens will be merciful towards you" (*Sunan Tirmidhi:* 1924; *Sunan Abu Daud*: 4941).

This *hadith* report very clearly expresses a basic Qur'anic teaching. The *Qur'an* states that the path to salvation is through showing mercy and love to others:

> And what will explain to thee, the path that is steep? (It is) freeing the bondman; Or the giving of food in a day of privation to the orphan with claims of relationship, or to the indigent (down) in the dust. Then will he be of those who believe, and enjoin patience, (constancy, and self-restraint), and enjoin deeds of kindness and compassion. (90:12–18)

This is the path of salvation—not simply to be kind-hearted, but also to participate in the mission to promote, in practical terms, kind-heartedness and compassion for others. Such are the steps on the path to salvation. Islam does not restrict good behaviour simply to other human beings. Rather, it insists that Muslims should behave in this way with all living creatures. Thus, according to a *hadith* recorded in the *Sahih* of al-Bukhari, the Prophet said, "There is merit (*sawab*) in behaving well towards all living creatures."

Bond of Common Nationality or Community

Islam recognizes a certain sort of brotherhood and feeling of bonding among members of the same community or nation as an established fact. This is expressed in the *Qur'an* in the form of various prophets, such as Hud, Saleh, Shoeb and so on, addressing the non-Muslim members of their communities as brothers, and, in this way, accepting a relationship of nation or community-based brotherhood between Muslims and non-Muslims belonging to the same nation or community. When these prophets of God preached His message to their own people (who were not Muslims, or 'submitters' to God), they addressed them as *ya qaum* or 'O my people', appealing to their hearts and reminding them of the common bond of community that they shared with them. This clearly indicates the sort of concern and love that Muslims should adopt when addressing their non-Muslim compatriots and seeking to cement bonds with them.

The importance of how concern and love should infuse relations between people belonging to the same race or origin despite their religious differences is evident from the fact that the Prophet Muhammad cared for the then non-Muslim Egyptians just because the mother of the Prophet Ishmael, son of the Prophet Abraham, and ancestor of the Arabs, was from Egypt. The Prophet instructed the Arabs to remember this ancient racial tie, saying that they would soon conquer Egypt and that he wanted them to deal with the Egyptians kindly because they had the right to protection (*haq-e zimma*) and because their racial ties with the Arabs demanded this.

Kind Behaviour with Non-Muslims: Some Examples

Various Islamic teachings indicate the kindness and concern that non-Muslims deserve from Muslims. The *Qur'an* mentions that needy non-Muslims are deserving of the financial assistance of Muslims, and that, therefore, they should be helped. In the *Qur'an,* God says that setting someone on the right path is not the work of human beings, and that God guides whom He wills. The *Qur'an* adds that we must not refuse to help a needy person simply because he or she refuses to accept Islam. It says that we shall be rewarded for whatever we spend in God's way:

> It is not required of thee (O Messenger) to set them on the right path but Allah guides to the right path whom He pleaseth. Whatever of good ye give benefits your own souls and ye shall only do so seeking the "Face" of Allah. Whatever good ye give, shall be rendered back to you and ye shall not be dealt with unjustly. (2:272)

This verse indicates that while providing financial help to others, it is not necessary to distinguish between those who accept Islam and those who do not. In other words, all needy people are deserving of such help.

Elaborating on this verse, the noted scholar Imam Ibn Jarir al-Tabari wrote in his *Tafsir* that this verse commands Muslims not to deprive non-Muslims of charity. He was of the view that this was how numerous companions of the Prophet and those who came after them in the next generation understood this verse. This was also the practice of the 'rightly-guided' caliphs. Thus, as mentioned in the *Kitab al-Kharaj* by Abu Yusuf, the Caliph Umar sent a letter to his governor, instructing him to provide for his poor and needy non-Muslim subjects from the wealth of the Muslims.

Kindness towards Relatives

Islam stresses kindness towards relatives, so much so that it says that God declares war against he who does not fulfill his responsibilities towards his relatives (*Musnad Ahmad:* 1684*; Sahih al-Bukhari*: 5987-5989). It also declares that those who sunder their ties with their relatives will have no place in heaven (*Sahih Muslim*: 2556).

Kindness towards, and reconciliation with, relatives applies to all relatives, Muslim as well as non-Muslim. It is their right. Islam seeks to cement relations, not to destroy them. Thus, non-Muslim relatives have all the rights over a Muslim so much so that the *Qur'an* lays down that if a Muslim's parents are not Muslim themselves, and even if they seek to pressurize their Muslim son or daughter to abandon Islam, they must be treated well under all conditions, although one should not yield to their pressure. As the *Qur'an* puts it:

> And We have enjoined on man (to be good) to his parents: in travail upon travail did his mother bear him, and in years twain was his weaning: (hear the command) "Show gratitude to Me and to thy parents: to Me is (thy final) Goal." But if they strive to make the join in worship with Me things of which thou hast no knowledge obey them not; Yet bear them company in this life with justice (and consideration) and follow the way of those who turn to Me (in love): in the End the return of you all is to Me, and I will tell you the truth (and meaning) of all that ye did (31:14–15).

The mother of Abu Hurairah, a companion of the Prophet, used to say bad things about the Prophet, but Abu Hurairah tolerated this. When he complained about her behaviour to the Prophet, the latter prayed for her, rather than expressing hatred for her. Because of this, she was guided (*Sahih Muslim:* 2491).

The mother of Asma, daughter of Abu Bakr, was a polytheist. In the wake of the Treaty of Hudaibiyah between the Muslims, led by the Prophet, and the Meccan pagans, relatives from both sides were able to meet each other. At this time, Asma's mother came to Medina to meet her, bringing along with her some gifts. Asma thought of reciprocating this gesture by giving her mother some presents when she was returning. However, she hesitated, not sure if Islam allowed for Muslims to present gifts to their non-Muslim relatives. Accordingly, she approached the Prophet and asked him if she should seek to strengthen her ties with her mother. In reply, the Prophet said she must indeed do so, and instructed her to give her gifts. (*Sahih al-Bukhari*: 2602).

Some commentators claim that Asma's mother had come to Medina because she was in need of financial help. But the fact is that she was a well-off woman, and Hafiz Ibn Hajar and other scholars have recorded such narrations that indicate that she herself had brought gifts for her daughter. Thus, it could be that she wanted to restore her bonds with her daughter that had earlier been sundered. In other words, Asma's giving gifts to her mother appears not to have been an expression of material help to a needy mother, but rather, a way of expressing and fulfilling her duty of familial love.

Other Social Relations between Muslims and Others

While Muslims have been forbidden to engage in such relations with non-Muslims that might undermine or destroy their religious distinctiveness, Islam stresses that

Muslims must relate with concern and a high standard of morality with non-Muslims in general in order to create a better society. Treating neighbours kindly is such an important Islamic teaching that in the corpus of *hadith* it has been said that not abiding by this can sometimes even lead to the danger of one's own faith being taken away. The Prophet thrice proclaimed that a person who is a source of discomfort to his neighbour is not a believer or *mumin* (*Sahih al-Bukhari*: 6016).

One's neighbour, who deserves exemplary treatment, can be both a Muslim or a non-Muslim, and the above-mentioned principle applies in both cases. This is well-illustrated in the following story. One day, a goat was slaughtered in the home of Abdullah (d 693 CE), a companion of the Prophet. He was a noted scholar of *hadith* and son of the Caliph Umar. When he returned home, the first thing he did was to ask if some of the meat had been sent to the house of his Jewish neighbour. 'I have heard the Prophet stressing the importance of kindness towards neighbours,' he said (*Sunan Abu Daud*: 5152).

From the life of the Prophet, which serves as a model for Muslims to emulate, we learn that even if an enemy is in great trouble, one should supplicate for him with God. On the one hand, the Prophet would beseech God to punish bloody oppressors, but, on the other hand, we see the Prophet helping the Quraish of Mecca, who stiffly opposed him, when they were faced with a severe famine. In that critical situation, Abu Sufian (d 650 CE), the Quraish leader, came to him. Invoking their relationship, he said that the Quraish, the tribe that the Prophet himself belonged to, were dying, and requested him to beseech God. The Prophet prayed to God, and because of his prayer the situation was cured (*Sahih al-Bukhari*: 4824).

If a Jew present in the Prophet's congregation would sneeze, the Prophet would make the same supplication (*du'a*), 'May God give you guidance and improve your condition', for him as he would for a Muslim (*Sunan Abu Daud*: 5040). Because they were so fond of this supplication, some Jews would pretend to sneeze, but the Prophet continued making this *du'a* for them. In the *Masannaf Ibn Abi Shaiba,* the *Masannaf Abdur Razzak* and the *Sahih al-Bukhari,* there are numerous narrations about the Prophet making *du'a* for non-Muslims. This clearly shows that Islam exhorts its followers to deal kindly with people of other faiths.

Commensality or eating together has great importance in building relationships. The Prophet used to invite non-Muslims for meals (*Al-Musnad*: 885). Expressing concern for the oppressed and distressed, irrespective of religion, is something basic for good social ties, and the Prophet Muhammad also abided by this. He would visit the homes of non-Muslims when they were sick to enquire about their health (*Sahih al-Bukhari*: 5657). He also gave gifts to non-Muslims, and courteously accepted the gifts that they presented him with, as has been recorded in the books of *hadith*.

It is narrated that a non-Muslim ruler once sent the Prophet a beautiful embroidered cloak, which he accepted (*Sahih al-Bukhari*: 2616). He gave it to his cousin Jafar Ibn Abi Talib (d 629 CE), saying that he should send it to his 'brother', Najashi, the ruler of Abyssinia, who had helped the Muslims (*Musnad Ahmad*: 13214). The Caliph Umar sent a valuable cloth as a gift to a 'polytheist brother' of his, and the Prophet knew about this (*Sahih Muslim*: 2068). The ruler of Aila once sent the Prophet a cloth and a mount, which were put to use (*Sahih al-Bukhari*: 3161). At the time when the Prophet was departing from this world, he instructed Muslims, especially their leaders, that the delegations of guests (and these would include non-Muslims) that would come to them should be given presents while departing, as he himself had done (*Sahih al-Bukhari*: 3053, *Sahih Muslim*: 1637).

From these references to the *Shari'ah* and the *sunnah*, the practice of the Prophet Muhammad, it is clear that Islam stands for humanitarianism, love, concern, compassion, large-heartedness, and good behaviour with people of other faiths in general. That is to say, if a person who follows another faith is not an oppressor or an enemy of Islam or a conspirator and is not engaged in war against Muslims, Islam considers him or her worthy of help and solidarity and stresses respect for his or her humanity.

Islamic Identity and Religious Differences Remain

While Islam stresses good relations with people of other faiths, it is also mindful of its distinctive teachings and of the fact that the aim of its true followers is not to wallow in worldly comforts. It does not permit its moral identity and principles to be sacrificed or diluted. It does not allow

Muslims to blindly imitate others so that the identity and distinctiveness of Islamic teachings and principles are wiped out. Islam does indeed call for unity and brotherly relations with people of other faiths, but not at the cost of the distinct identity of the Muslims. It cannot allow Muslims to lose their identity by being absorbed into another community.

For a person or a community to be 'Muslim' naturally means to regard the Islamic way of life and the commandments of God and the Prophet Muhammad to be true and just, and to consider all practices opposed to these commands as wrong and as something to be abstained from. Because today many people have lost their moral sense, some consider adherence to this principle as akin to extremism, although this is precisely what adherence to any principle is all about. This applies not just to Islam but, rather, to all missionary movements.

According to a *hadith* report, the Prophet warned Muslims against imitating or following the ways of other communities. This issue has been incorrectly understood by some people. The actual import of this *hadith* is to warn Muslims from adopting or imitating those aspects of the identity of other communities that relate to the latter's religious and social distinctiveness and with regard to which they are completely different from Muslims. It is obvious that a community that imitates or adopts such customs and practices associated with another community would soon be overwhelmed by the latter and be made to feel inferior, and that it would gradually begin to lose its own identity, finally ending up being absorbed into the community whose ways it imitates.

According to the *Kanz al-Daqaiq*, a text of Hanafi Muslim jurisprudence, Muslims are not forbidden from adopting all the customs or practices of the People of the Book—Jews and Christians. Only those things are forbidden for Muslims to imitate or adopt that are unlawful (*haram*) or wrong. Muslims are also not allowed to adopt any practice with the intention of becoming like them. The same argument has been made by Imam Abu Yusuf (d 798 CE), the noted Hanafi jurisprudent, as quoted in the *Durr ul-Mukhtar*, a well-known text on Hanafi law.

It is evident from this that this restriction does not aim at promoting hatred for, or enmity against, others, but rather at protecting the Muslims' ideological and moral distinctiveness. Nor does it aim to promote a narrow communal consciousness and false sense of communal superiority among Muslims. This restriction should be viewed in the light of the fact that Islam has provided its adherents a set of religious principles, moral values, and beliefs, on the basis of which they should lead their lives. In order to protect their faith, beliefs, and lifestyle, it stresses the need for them to express their distinctiveness from others in certain matters, while at the same time insisting that Muslims should seek to cultivate kind brotherly relations with them. This distinctiveness is needed in order to protect the Muslims from being absorbed or assimilated into other communities as a result of close interaction, which might otherwise cause them to lose their own identity.

While Islam exhorts Muslims to establish close and cordial relations with non-Muslims in general, it forbids them from collaborating with those non-Muslim enemies of Islam who are bent on the destruction of Islam, who are at war with Muslims, or who are engaged in dangerous conspiracies against them. For, as the *Qur'an* says:

> O ye who believe! Take not My enemies and yours as friends (or protectors)—offering them (your) love, even though they

> have rejected the Truth that has come to you, and have (on the contrary) driven out the Messenger and yourselves (from your homes), (simply) because ye believe in Allah your Lord! If ye have come out to strive in My Way and to seek My Good Pleasure (take them not as friends), holding secret converse of love (and friendship) with them: for I know full well all that ye conceal and all that ye reveal. And any of you that does this has strayed from the Straight Path. If they were to get the better of you, they would behave to you as enemies, and stretch forth their hands and their tongues against you for evil; and they desire that ye should reject the Truth. (60:1–2)

Serious Misunderstanding

The question is often raised that while Muslims often claim that Islam teaches them to live at peace with people of other faiths and to relate with them with kindness, love and concern, the reality is just the opposite, because, it is alleged, the *Qur'an* prohibits Muslims from having social or other such relations with non-Muslims and prohibits friendship with them.

This wrong allegation is based on two basic misunderstandings. Firstly, an erroneous understanding of the terms *wali* and *wala* used in the *Qur'an*. Secondly, misunderstanding of precisely which group of unbelievers this prohibition applies to. In this regard, the fact is often ignored that at several places, the *Qur'an* qualifies its statements so as to indicate that this prohibition does not apply to all non-Muslims in general, but rather to only a particular type among them. At one place, the *Qur'an* also explicitly mentions that this prohibition applies just to a particular group among the non-Muslims, and that friendship with other non-Muslims is not forbidden. As the *Qur'an* very clearly puts it:

> Allah does not forbid you to deal justly and kindly with those who fought not against you on account of religion nor drove you out of your homes, verily Allah loves who deal with equity. Allah forbids you only regarding those who have fought you on account of Religion, and have expelled you from your homes, and have given support in your expulsion, that you should take them for friends; and whoso takes them for friends and helpers, those are the wrong-doers. (60:8–9)

First Misunderstanding

The first misunderstanding arises from a misreading of certain verses of the *Qur'an* that forbid Muslims from taking disbelievers as their *walis*. The Arabic word *wali* has been wrongly taken to be the synonymous of 'friend'. In actual fact, there is no strict equivalent of the Arabic word *al-wali* or its derivatives in Urdu and English and many other languages. That is why it is often rendered simply as *dost* in Urdu and 'friend' in English. It is this that causes people to wrongly believe that Islam forbids Muslims from taking non-Muslims as their friends.

The word *wali* actually refers to a person with whom one has a very intimate friendship. This also connotes helping, assisting and being in solidarity with such a person. Imam Ibn Jarir Tabari, a noted Qur'anic commentator who was an expert in the Arabic language as well, explains a verse in the *Qur'an* that ordains, 'Let not the believers take for (*wali*) friends or helpers unbelievers against the believers (3: 28)' as follows: "In this verse, God has forbidden the true believers from taking the disbelievers as their *wali* (helpers)."

Explaining this verse, and particularly the term *wali*, he further comments that this means they are 'forbidden from considering them as their supporters, assisting them in their religion, supporting them against the Muslims and the true believers, and sharing the secrets of the Muslims with them'. Commenting on the use of a derivative of the term *wali* in the *Qur'an*, he adds, 'In the Arabic language, the general meaning of the word *wali* is helper and supporter.'

From this discussion, it is evident that these verses forbid Muslims from establishing secret ties with the disbelievers or to assist them surreptitiously. These verses have nothing to do with forbidding friendship and good relations with non-Muslims in general. This is made even more clear when the *Qur'an* explains that the *wala* or close bonding that it forbids is that which denotes 'help against the true believers' (for instance, *Surah Aal-e Imra*n: 28; *Surah An-Nisa*: 139 and 144). This restriction or specification regarding the phrase 'against the true believers' itself indicates that the bonding that the *Qur'an* forbids is of that sort that entails helping disbelievers against the Muslims.

The precise context of these verses, which is clearly evident in the verses themselves, must be properly understood. Without this, their actual import is likely to be misunderstood. The disbelievers that they refer to, whom the *Qur'an* forbids Muslims from closely bonding with and helping, were those who were determined to wipe out Islam and were involved in a massive campaign for this purpose. They had even unleashed war against the Muslims. These included the polytheists of Mecca as well as the Jews of Medina. Besides engaging in war against the Muslims, they also sought to spread internal dissension, conflict, and inter-tribal disputes among them, and routinely vilified

Islam and the Prophet.

At that time, Muslims had blood relatives and friends among both the polytheists of Mecca and the Jews of Medina. They had social relations and dealings with them. A number of hypocrites (*munafiqin*) among the Muslims also sympathized with the Meccan polytheists and the Medinan Jews, and they proved to be cunning agents of the opponents of Islam in their conspiracies. The *Qur'an* unveiled the dangerous activities of this group of people. These subversive activities had reached such a dangerous point that in the ninth year of the Islamic calendar, the hypocrites set up their own centre, calling it a mosque, at Quba, whose aim was to undermine and destroy the polity at Medina headed by the Prophet, instigate dissensions among the Muslims, invite an army from outside to invade the town, and fan internal revolt. This is what the *Qur'an* uncovered (see *Surah At-Tauba*: 107).

Besides these inveterate hypocrites, there was also a group of people among the Muslims with weak faith, who used to oscillate between the Muslims and their opponents, depending on which way the wind was blowing. The hypocrites were, by and large, under the influence of the Medinan Jews, and were working to fulfill their agenda (see *Surah Al-Maida*: 52).

The *Qur'an* instructed the Prophet to warn these hypocrites to be ready to be punished in Hell for having established secret relations with the enemies of Islam. It is in this context that the *Qur'an* berates them for choosing disbelievers as their *walis* and for leaving aside the true believers in the mistaken expectation that, in this way, they could acquire respect and power. They sat along with the leaders of the disbelieving foes of Islam in their meetings, where the latter would mock Islam and the Prophet. The *Qur'an* says that these hypocrites used to remain in waiting, being neither fully with the Muslims nor fully with their enemies, so that if the Muslims were victorious, they could come to them, saying that they were with them, and that if the disbelievers triumphed, they could go to them, saying that they had assisted them in defeating the Muslims.

This behaviour of the hypocrites is what the *Qur'an* refers to when it forbids the believers from taking disbelievers as their *walis*. As mentioned above, this group of hypocrites was heavily under the social and political influence of the Jews, and was hand-in-glove with them in their scurrilous propaganda against Islam and the Prophet. The *Qur'an* refers to this situation (particularly in *Surah Al-Ahzab* and *Surah An-Noor*).

The leaders of the Jews mocked and reviled Islam, and in their meetings, some Muslims would also be present. The pagan Arabs were also involved in this. These Jews and pagan Arabs tried to incite ordinary Muslims to disobey the Prophet and revolt against him. It was in this context that the *Qur'an* says that those in whose hearts there is a disease (that is to say, the hypocrites) rush towards the disbelievers to join hands with them for fear that otherwise they might fall into trouble.

This is the sort of *wala* or solidarity (a term related to the word *wali*) with the enemies of Islam who are bent on uprooting Islam that the *Qur'an* forbids. Obviously, a relationship of *wala* with such people would be a direct contradiction of one's Islamic faith, as well as a grave threat to Muslims at the political and social levels.

Second Misunderstanding

Another cause of considerable misunderstanding about Islam's teachings with regard to the permissibility or otherwise of friendship between Muslims and others is that the above-mentioned prohibition of *wala*, or taking disbelievers as *walis*, has been erroneously interpreted as applying to all non-Muslims in general. It must be stressed here that, as the discussion of various Qur'anic verses above has shown, this order applies only to those non-Muslims who are enemies of Islam and who are involved in activities aimed at undermining and destroying it. This point is strikingly brought out in the following verses of the *Qur'an*:

> O ye who believe! Take not into your intimacy those outside your ranks: They will not fail to corrupt you. They only desire your ruin: Rank hatred has already appeared from their mouths: What their hearts conceal is far worse. We have made plain to you the Signs, if ye have wisdom. Ah! Ye are those who love them, but they love you not—though ye believe in the whole of the Book. When they meet you, they say, "We believe": But when they are alone, they bite off the very tips of their fingers at you in their rage. Say: "Perish in your rage; Allah knoweth well all the secrets of the heart." If aught that is good befalls you, it grieves them; but if some misfortune overtakes you, they rejoice at it. But if ye are constant and do right, not the least harm will their cunning do to you; for Allah Compasseth round about all that they do. (3:118–120)

These verses specifically refer to those whose hearts burn with enmity and who are engaged in plots to destroy the Muslims. It does not refer to ordinary, well-meaning, kind and sincere people of other faiths. The true import of these commandments can be properly understood from the fact that in a very highly secretive and sensitive matter, the migration of the Prophet from Mecca to Medina, the Prophet not only shared his plans with a non-Muslim, Abdullah ibn Arqad, but also fully trusted him, and took him as a guide in his journey of the *hijrah*. This fact clearly suggests that these verses forbid taking as confidants and intimates only those non-Muslims who are enemies of Islam and its followers.

It is thus obvious and needs no explanation that a non-Muslim of good character is much better to have as a friend than a person who is Muslim in name alone and is actually a hypocrite and an opportunist.

The sort of non-Muslims that the *Qur'an* forbids Muslims from taking as their intimate associates is clearly indicated in the following verse:

> O ye who believe! Take not My enemies and yours as friends [or protectors]—offering them (your) love, even though they have rejected the Truth that has come to you, and have (on the contrary) driven out the Messenger and yourselves (from your homes), (simply) because ye believe in Allah your Lord! If ye have come out to strive in My Way and to seek My Good Pleasure (take them not as friends), holding secret converse of

> love (and friendship) with them: for I know full well all that ye conceal and all that ye reveal. And any of you that does this has strayed from the Straight Path. If they were to get the better of you, they would behave to you as enemies, and stretch forth their hands and their tongues against you for evil; and they desire that ye should reject the Truth. (60:1–2)

This verse strongly and explicitly forbids Muslims from taking disbelievers as their *walis*, but here too it does not refer to all non-Muslims in general. Rather, it refers only to those who are enemies of God and the Muslims and who 'have driven out the Messenger and yourselves (from your homes), (simply) because ye believe in Allah your Lord'.

Precisely which non-Muslims this Qur'anic prohibition applies to is thus a crucial issue that needs to be carefully understood. Conversely, we must also properly understand which non-Muslims this prohibition does not apply to. The *Qur'an* very clearly indicates that this prohibition does not apply to the general non-Muslims who relate with peace and goodwill with Muslims. Instead, it restricts this prohibition only to those non-Muslims who are enemies of Islam and the Muslims. Thus, the *Qur'an* relates:

> Allah forbids you not, with regard to those who fight you not for (your) Faith nor drive you out of your homes, from dealing

> kindly and justly with them: for Allah loveth those who are just. Allah only forbids you, with regard to those who fight you for (your) Faith, and drive you out of your homes, and support (others) in driving you out, from turning to them (for friendship and protection). It is such as turn to them (in these circumstances) that do wrong. (60:8–9)

These verses very explicitly show precisely what sort of non-Muslims the Muslims have been prohibited by the *Qur'an* to take as their *walis*, and, on the other hand, which non-Muslims this prohibition does not apply to. From this discussion, it is clear that Muslims can, indeed, take ordinary non-Muslims, who do not bear any enmity against Islam and its adherents and who are not engaged in any activities against them, as their friends.

Critique of False Position

The above discussion clearly shows that the arguments of some people who claim that Muslims must never befriend non-Muslims and that such friendship is banned in Islam are completely wrong. These people have not understood the relevant Qur'anic verses in their totality. Thus, for instance, Shaikh Muhammad Ibn Abdul Wahhab (d 1792 CE), founder of a reformist movement in Arabia, later known as the Wahhabi movement, even went to the extent of claiming that 'a Muslim's faith in Islam cannot be proper, even if he believes in one God and has abandoned polytheism, till he harbours enmity for the polytheists.' Likewise, a contemporary Saudi Islamic scholar, Dr Sahl Ibn Rifa-ah al-Utaibi, who teaches Islamic theology at the Ibn Saud University, Riyadh, claims that 'Islam has forbidden love for non-Muslims, but still instructs them to deal with them with kindness.' He argues this on the basis of his own reading of the following two Qur'anic verses:

> Thou will not find any people who believe in Allah and the Last Day, loving those who resist Allah and His Messenger, even though they were their fathers or their sons, or their brothers, or their kindred. (58–22)

and

> O ye who believe! Take not My enemies and yours as friends and protectors—offering them (your) love, even though they have rejected the Truth that has come to you, and have (on the contrary) driven out the Messenger and yourselves (from your homes), (simply) because ye believe in Allah your Lord! (60:1)

It is obvious, however, that Dr al-Utabi's argument and reasoning are faulty. Neither of the above-mentioned two verses deals with non-Muslims in general. The first verse refers only to those non-Muslims who have waged war against God and His Prophet and are enemies of Islam. The second verse also refers to the same sort of people. Besides, the general context of these two verses also clarifies that it is only this sort of non-Muslims—and not all non-Muslims in general—that the verses refer to.

It is true that Islam is sternly opposed to polytheism and infidelity and the ways of life based on them. But this certainly does not mean that Islam commands Muslims to hate all non-Muslims. It certainly does not order Muslims not to love, on the basis of their common humanity or common race and community, those non-Muslims who are peaceful and well-meaning. From the above-quoted verses, it is evident that the *Qur'an* orders Muslims to deal justly and kindly with non-Muslims who wish to live at peace with them and who do not oppress them. The *Qur'an* instructs Muslims to entertain good and noble feelings for such people, to be concerned about them, to work for their welfare, to be compassionate towards them, and to help them in times of need.

The words of Shaikh Muhammad Ibn Abdul Wahhab that I earlier quoted, which drip with extremism, are echoed by another Saudi scholar, the late Mufti of Saudi Arabia, Shaikh Abdul Aziz Ibn Baz (d 1999) in a letter he wrote in response to an article by the former rector of Al-Azhar, Shaikh Jad ul-Haq. The latter had insisted on not just good relations between Muslims and others, but also cooperation with them in religious matters, considering Islam, Christianity and Judaism as partners sharing common values. He had written, 'Muslims consider the followers of Judaism and Christianity as believers in God and divinely-revealed religions. There is no difference among them as regards the basic principles of their Divine message.' This claim is incorrect because it denies the basic differences between Islam and other religions.

Today's Christianity and Judaism have departed far from their true, original forms, and so cannot be said to be the same in their basic principles as Islam. Ibn Baz pointed this fact out, but he went to another extreme by wrongly claiming, "Undoubtedly, God has made it incumbent upon the believers to hate, and to be enemies with, the disbelievers and has forbidden them from loving them" (*Fatawa Shaikh Ibn Baz*: 8/91).

It is obvious that this argument is erroneous. It represents a gross misinterpretation or misunderstanding of Islamic teachings. There is no basis for such a claim in the *Qur'an*. Rather, there are enough references in the *Qur'an* to challenge and refute this argument. It is necessary to urgently critique and to do away with these wrong interpretations.

*

All praise be to God! I hope that this book has been able to appropriately explain the Islamic concept of jihad and that it has also been able to clear the numerous misunderstandings about this doctrine that abound today.